GRAMMAR RULES!

Second edition

Tanya Gibb

STUDENT BOOK 4

Grammar in the real world

Name: ______________________________

Class: ______________________________

macmillan education

Note to teachers and parents

Grammar Rules!

Grammar Rules! comprehensively meets the requirements of the Australian Curriculum English. The scope and sequence outlined on pages 4–5 integrates Language, Literature and Literacy to develop students' knowledge, understanding and skills in listening, reading, viewing, speaking and representing.

Grammar Rules! also supports the New Zealand English Curriculum strands: Listening, Reading and Viewing; and Speaking, Writing and Presenting. Students will use processes and strategies to develop knowledge, skills and understandings, related to purposes and audiences, ideas, language features and structure.

Grammar can be defined as the way language is organised to make meaning. Knowledge of the grammatical features that make language use more effective is vital for all students. They need an understanding of grammar to be able to make appropriate choices to get their message across in speaking and writing (creating texts); and they need to know how to analyse the language used by others when they are listening and reading (interpreting texts). Grammatical knowledge will assist students to become analytical, critical and evaluative language users.

Grammar Rules! shows students how grammatical structures and features function in texts to achieve meaning, from the contextual level of the whole text down to sentence level and to the level of words and word parts. The series explains appropriate grammatical structures for particular types of texts, language functions and social purposes. The second edition of the *Grammar Rules!* program also incorporates elements of self-assessment. A simple reflection activity allows students to assess their own progress and provides you with a starting point for discussion.

Student Book 4

Units of work

Student Book 4 contains 35 weekly units of work presented in a conceptually sound scope and sequence. The intention is for students to work through the units in the sequence in which they are presented. See the **Scope and Sequence Chart** on pages 4–5 for more information. There are also regular Revision Units that can be used for consolidation or assessment purposes.

The sample texts in *Student Book 4* are based around the theme of water. The subject matter of the sample texts is not tied to any particular content across other curriculum areas. This allows teachers and students to focus on the way language is structured according to purpose and audience. Students can then use this knowledge to evaluate, respond to and create texts in other learning areas. The concepts in the sample texts link well with the Cross-Curriculum Priority of Sustainability, as well the General Capabilities of Critical and Creative Thinking, Personal and Social Capability, Ethical Understanding and Intercultural Understanding, as described in the Australian Curriculum.

Icons

Encourages students to create texts of their own to demonstrate their understanding of the grammatical concepts taught in the unit. These activities focus on written language; however, many also provide opportunities for using spoken language to engage with others, make presentations and develop skills in using ICT.

Highlights useful grammatical rules and concepts. The rule is always introduced the first time students need it to complete an activity.

Tells students that a special hint is provided for an activity. It might be a tip about language functions, or a reminder to look at a rule in a previous unit.

Allows students to assess their progress through each unit.

Grammar Rules Glossary

A valuable glossary is provided at the end of *Student Book 4*. Teachers and students can use this as a straightforward dictionary of grammar terminology, or as a summary of important grammar rules used in *Student Book 4*. Page references are also given for the point in the book where the rule was first introduced, so that students can go back to that unit if they need more information or further revision of the rule.

Pull-Out Writing Log

At the centre of *Student Book 4* is a practical pull-out Writing Log so that students can directly relate the grammar they learn back to their own writing. Students could store the Writing Log in their writing folders, and use it to keep track of the grammar, language functions and types of texts they use. The Writing Log also includes a handy reminder of the writing process, as well as a checklist of types of texts and text forms for students to try.

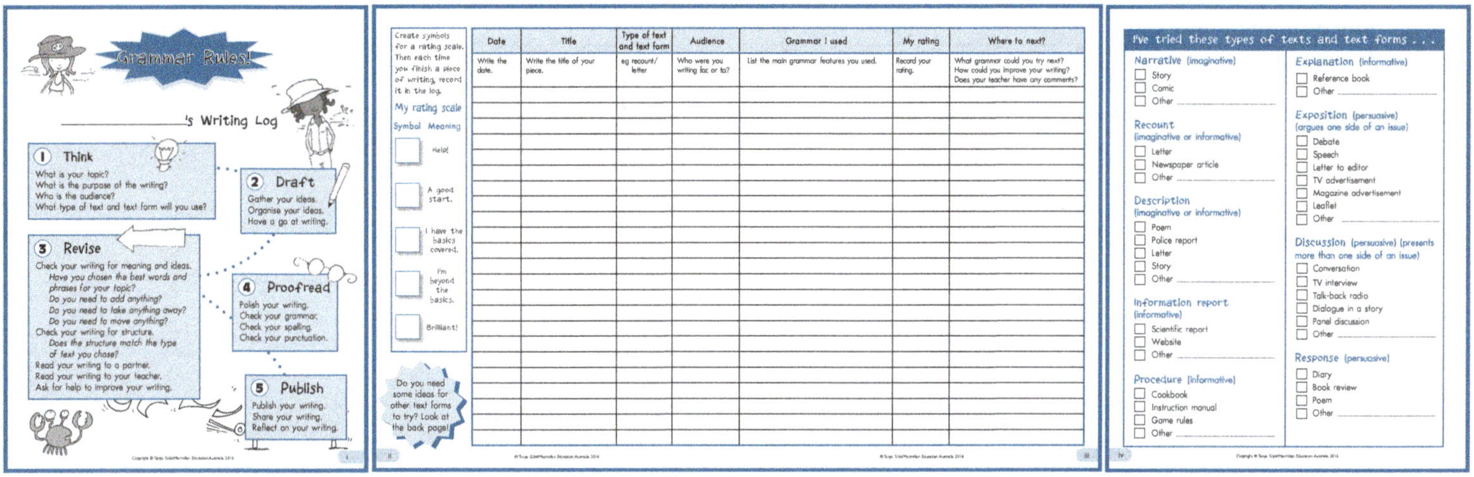

Unit at a Glance

Unit tag
States the main grammar focus

Text sample
Illustrates the grammar focus at work, in the real context of a specific type of text

Sequenced activities
Each activity focuses on a specific aspect of grammar

Tip!
Reminds or gives a special hint

Type of text description
Highlights the type of text, and purpose and grammar focus of the sample text

Rule!
Introduces students to a new concept

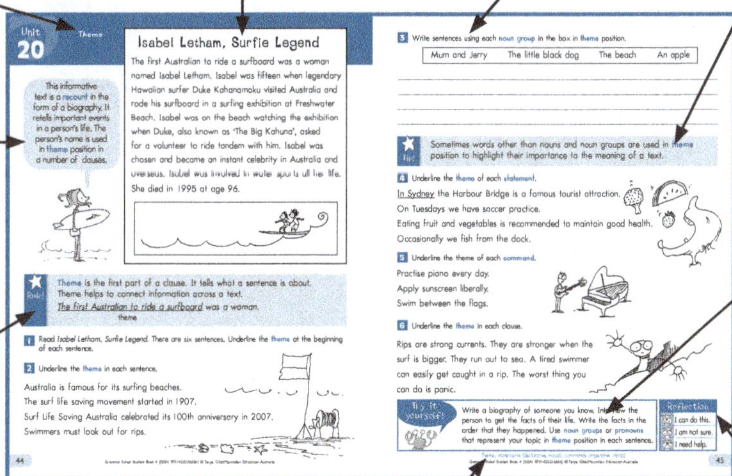

Try it yourself!
Gives students the opportunity to apply grammar in the context of their own texts using the sample texts as models. Provides opportunities for planning, drafting and editing texts and using software and word processing programs to publish them

Footer
Lists the full grammar focus covered in the unit

Reflection
Allows students to assess their progress

Grammar Rules! Teacher Resource Book 3–6

Full teacher support for *Student Book 4* is provided by *Grammar Rules! Teacher Resource Book 3–6*. Here you will find valuable background information about grammar, along with practical resources, such as:

- ☆ strategies for teaching grammar
- ☆ grammar games and activities
- ☆ assessment strategies
- ☆ teaching tips for every unit in *Student Book 4*
- ☆ answers for every unit in *Student Book 4*

Scope and Sequence

This scope and sequence chart is based on the requirements of the Australian Curriculum.

Unit	Unit name/ Type of text	Clause to whole text level			Word and word group level		
		Sentences and clauses	Cohesion: theme, pronouns, lexical chains, connectives	Mood and modality, language and vocabulary	Nouns and noun groups	Verbs and verb groups	Adverbs and prepositional phrases
1	Dear Timmy Recount/Email				nouns	past tense doing verbs	
2	My Day at the Beach Recount				proper and common nouns	past tense saying verbs	
3	The Big Catch Narrative		conjunctions (connectives): *so, but, because*			thinking and feeling verbs	
4	Dear Diary Recount/Diary		personal pronouns: *me, I, we, us*		noun groups		
5	A Tale of Little Fish Narrative		personal pronouns		noun groups		
6	REVISION						
7	Kakadu Seasons Description/Poem				noun groups; descriptive adjectives		
8	Our New Dam Recount		personal pronouns: *we, I*		noun groups including number adjectives, singular and plural nouns, collective nouns		
9	Dear Mum Recount/Email		possessive pronouns		possessive adjectives; apostrophes to show possession		
10	Australia's Mightiest River System Information report	simple sentences		technical vocabulary		relating verbs (being and having verbs): *is, belongs, equals, was, had, are*	
11	The Driest Place on Earth Information report	clauses	conjunctions (connectives): *and, so, because*	questions and statements; technical vocabulary; question words			
12	REVISION						
13	Under the Sea Description/Illustration						prepositions: *in, on, under, over, beside, off, with, near, during, after, at, before, from, inside;* prepositional phrases
14	Frog Potion Procedure/Recipe			commands	noun groups with prepositional phrases	doing verbs	prepositional phrases
15	How to Catch a Fish Procedure/Instructions			commands		doing verbs	adverbs to tell how
16	Sun Safety Procedure/Instructions				noun groups	verb tense	
17	Directions to the Olympic Pool Procedure/Instructions			commands	proper nouns	doing verbs	
18	REVISION						

Unit	Unit name/ Type of text	Clause to whole text level			Word and word group level		
		Sentences and clauses	Cohesion: theme, pronouns, lexical chains, connectives	Mood and modality, language and vocabulary	Nouns and noun groups	Verbs and verb groups	Adverbs and prepositional phrases
19	**Super Crab** Narrative/Comic strip	quoted (direct) speech; reported (indirect) speech					
20	**Isabel Letham, Surfie Legend** Recount/Biography		theme	statements; commands			
21	**Recycled Water** Explanation			technical vocabulary		verb tense; verb groups; helping verbs	
22	**We Tank You** Advertisement		personal pronouns;	commands		doing verbs in theme position	
23	**Lake Eyre** Information report	compound sentences	personal pronoun *it*; conjunctions (connectives): *however, so, and*	technical vocabulary	comparative and superlative adjectives		
24	REVISION						
25	**Sewage** Information report		lexical chains	technical vocabulary	commas in noun lists		
26	**How a Pearl is Made** Explanation		conjunctions (connectives to show cause and effect, to show time sequence)	technical vocabulary		verb groups; helping verbs; verb tense	
27	**Cane Toads** Information report		reference chains; theme position		classifying adjectives; proper nouns		
28	**What's Your Favourite Sea Animal?** Discussion/Interview transcript		conjunctions (connectives to show cause and effect, to compare and contrast)	question tags		thinking and feeling verbs	
29	**Daintree** Response/Travel review	compound sentences			noun groups with adjectives, subject verb agreement	thinking and feeling verbs	
30	REVISION						
31	**Tsunami** Information report			technical vocabulary		verb groups; regular and irregular verbs	adverbs
32	**High Tide Sends Residents to the Roof** Newspaper article	direct (quoted) speech; indirect (reported) speech		modality; emotive language		modal verbs: *will, will not, might, might not, should, should not*	
33	**Vote Against School Swimming** Exposition		connectives: *firstly, secondly, in addition*	modality		modal verbs: *might, should, could, must;* thinking and feeling verbs	
34	**Bobby and the Quest for the Hidden Treasure** Narrative		varying themes				prepositional phrases to tell when and where; adverbs to tell how
35	REVISION						

Unit 1

Nouns, doing verbs

This informative text is an email. It uses **nouns** and **past tense verbs** to **recount** an event.

Dear Timmy,

Last weekend I went fishing with my grandparents. We fished from the end of the jetty not far from where they live. My grandma caught the first fish. It was only small so she threw it back. I caught the second fish. My grandma shouted "Way to go, Milly!" My fish was too small to keep so I kissed it and let it go. My grandpa didn't catch anything but he didn't mind. We bought fish and chips on the way home. I like going fishing with my grandparents.

From Milly.

Rule! **Nouns** are words for people, places, animals or things.

1 Read *Dear Timmy*. Write the **nouns** used for these people, places, animals or things.

the people ______________________________

a place to stand and fish ______________________________

a place to live ______________________________

the food they ate ______________________________

2 In the following sentences, underline ten **nouns**.

Grandma lived in a caravan.

Dad cooked noodles.

I stood on the footpath.

The children rode bikes to school.

We saw dolphins in the waves.

3 Circle the **noun** in each row.

mum	jump	hop	skip
eat	beach	ate	licked
sand	kiss	yell	drag
swim	swam	float	bird
listen	talk	ice	speak

Rule! **Doing verbs** tell the actions. Sometimes the way a verb is written lets you know that the action happened in the past. This is called **past tense**.

4 Underline the **past tense doing verbs**.

I jumped over the fence.

Dad cooked dinner.

Mum fixed my bike.

He swam slowly.

She walked swiftly.

5 Write the **past tense** forms for each **doing verb**. Hint! You'll find them all in *Dear Timmy*.

fish ______________

catch ______________

throw ______________

kiss ______________

buy ______________

6 Change the form of the **doing verb** in brackets, so that the event happened in the past.

I (ride) ______________ a bike to school.

We (eat) ______________ apples for morning tea.

Mum (buys) ______________ bananas at the fruit market.

Grandpa (bounces) ______________ the basketball.

7 Choose a **past tense doing verb** from the box to complete each sentence.

made	chased	sailed	ate	ran

We ______________ lunch in the park.

Dad ______________ our sandwiches.

The yacht ______________ into the harbour.

The dog ______________ into the yard and ______________ the bird.

Try it yourself!

Write your own **recount** about something that happened to you last weekend. Use **nouns** for people, places and things. Remember to use the **past tense** forms of the **verbs**.

Reflection

I can do this.

I am not sure.

I need help.

Unit 2

Common and proper nouns, saying verbs

This informative text is a **recount**. It uses **proper nouns** for names of particular people and places.

My Day at the Beach

Last Saturday I went to Sandy Bay beach with my family. As soon as we got there I slathered on my sunscreen and went for a swim. After a while the waves started to get really rough so I helped my sister build a sandcastle. When it started to get cold, Mum announced it was time to leave. We shook off all the sand and got in the car. On the way home we stopped for ice-creams. Mine was strawberry-flavoured. It was really yummy!

1 Read *My Day at the Beach*. Write the **nouns** used for people, places and things.

people ______________________________

places ______________________________

things ______________________________

Rule!

Proper nouns are the names of particular people, places, animals or things. They begin with a capital letter.

Saturday Stephen March Australia

Common nouns are everyday naming words.

jetty fish day boat

2 Rewrite the sentences using capital letters for the **proper nouns**.

Did jasmine and daniel have a holiday in darwin?

____

I hope maria can come to my party on wednesday.

____

My birthday is in march and nellie's birthday is in may.

____

3 Write **common nouns** for things you can see.

at the beach ______________________________

in your car ______________________________

at an ice-cream shop ______________________________

in your kitchen ______________________________

Rule! **Saying verbs** are verbs that show that something is being said.

4 In *My Day at the Beach*, Mum *announced* that it was time to leave. Underline the **saying verbs**.

said	yelled	jumped	called	thought	stated

5 Write a **saying verb** on each line.

Mum ______________ , "Hurry up, we're late for school!"

"I want one too!" ______________ my little brother.

"Let's get out of here," ______________ Jessie.

"Where are we?" ______________ Lou.

6 Write sentences using the words in the box as **saying verbs**.

chuckled	reminded	meowed	screamed

____

____

____

____

Try it yourself!

Write a **recount** of a conversation you had with someone recently. Remember to write the **past tense** forms of **saying verbs** to show your conversation happened in the past. Remember that people's names are **proper nouns**.

Reflection

- I can do this.
- I am not sure.
- I need help.

Unit 3 Thinking and feeling verbs, conjunctions

The Big Catch

Joe loved sharks. He thought they were fascinating animals. He wanted to study them when he was older. Joe was excited today because, at long last, his uncle had agreed to let him go on his boat during a shark-tagging expedition. Joe had been nagging for months but his uncle had always claimed that being on a shark-tagging boat was too dangerous for a ten-year-old boy. Joe desperately hoped that today his uncle would be able to catch, tag and release a great white shark. Joe would quickly photograph it before it was released back into the ocean.

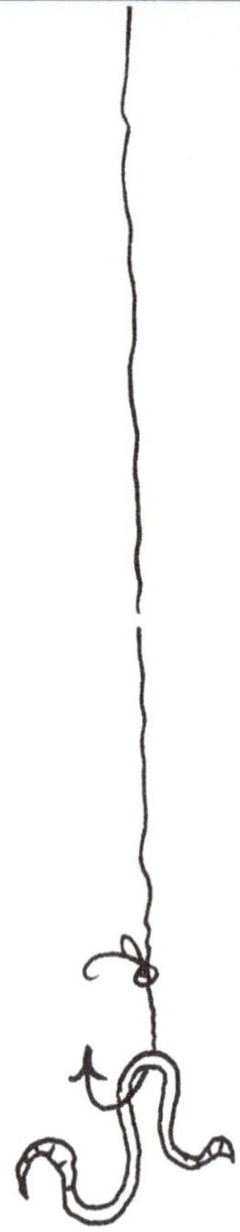

This imaginative text is the opening paragraph of a **narrative**. It uses **thinking and feeling verbs** to introduce the main character.

Rule! **Thinking and feeling verbs** represent mental activities, such as loving, hoping and believing. You can't see these activities taking place.

1 Circle the **thinking and feeling verbs** in the sentences.

Joe thought sharks were fascinating.

I think Joe cares for animals.

Joe's uncle wonders how many sharks he'll tag.

2 Write **thinking and feeling verbs** from the box to complete each sentence.

hoped	loved	felt	worried

Joe ________________ sharks.

Joe's uncle ________________ about Joe's safety.

Joe ________________ they'd tag a shark.

Joe ________________ proud that his uncle had an important job.

Rule!

Conjunctions are words that link ideas in a sentence.

Joe was happy <u>because</u> they tagged a great white shark.

3 Join the following sentences using the **conjunctions** in the box. Write the new sentences on the lines.

so	because	because	but

I like carrots. I don't like pumpkin.

____

It rained all day. We had to play inside.

____

I won the spelling contest. I studied hard.

____

I invited Ludmilla to my party. She is my friend.

____

4 Finish each sentence.

Joe likes sharks because ___________________________

Joe behaved well on the trip so ___________________________

They caught a bull shark but ___________________________

The weather was fine but ___________________________

Joe's uncle decided to take Joe because ___________________________

Joe took a photo so ___________________________

Try it yourself!

Write an orientation for a story. Use **thinking and feeling verbs** to represent the way the characters think and feel. Ask a peer to help edit your work.

Reflection

- I can do this.
- I am not sure.
- I need help.

Unit 4

Noun groups, personal pronouns

This informative text is a diary entry. It **recounts** events in a time sequence.

Dear Diary,

Yesterday our school held its annual swimming carnival. I was excited because I swam in three events. My first event was a twenty-five metre medley relay. I swam the backstroke leg. We came third. Next I had a twenty-five metre backstroke race. I finished first! I felt really proud when our school principal, Ms Ng, shook my hand and gave me a medal. My last event was freestyle. I'm pretty hopeless at freestyle but I tried my hardest and came fifth. I think I did a really good job at the carnival. I can't wait for next year.

Rule! A **noun group** is a group of words that contains a noun. The other words in the group tell more about the noun.

We ate my deliciously moist birthday cake.

1 Read *Dear Diary*. Write the **noun groups** used for these **nouns**.

relay ______________________

race ______________________

carnival ______________________

Ms Ng ______________________

2 Write **noun groups** of your own for each **noun** in the box.

kitten	friend	game

____

____

____

Rule!

Pronouns replace nouns.
Personal pronouns replace nouns for people and things.
Personal pronouns stand for the speaker or writer of the text.
me *I* *we* *us*

3 Circle the **personal pronouns** used in *Dear Diary*.

4 Use each **personal pronoun** in a sentence.

I	me	we	us

____

____

____

____

Tip!

I and *me* can be tricky when you are talking about yourself and someone else. To choose the correct **personal pronoun** follow this pattern:
I went to the shop. → *Ben and I went to the shop.*
Mum bought me a cake. → *Mum bought Ben and me cakes.*

5 Join the following sentences correctly, using either **me** or **I**.

Jai ate an apple. I ate an apple. Jai and ______ ate apples.

Dad helped me. Dad helped Debbie. Dad helped Debbie and ______.

Mum took my brother to the movies. Mum took me to the movies.
Mum took my brother and ______ to the movies.

Try it yourself!

Write a **recount** in the form of a diary entry about something exciting that has happened to you recently. Use the **personal pronouns** *me*, *I*, *we* and *us*.

Reflection
- I can do this.
- I am not sure.
- I need help.

Unit **5**

Noun groups, personal pronouns

This imaginative text is the orientation of a **narrative**. It uses **noun groups** to represent characters, places and things. It uses **personal pronouns** to refer to characters.

A Tale of Little Fish

A long time ago, in the depths of the deep, dark ocean, there lived a school of tiny, jittery fish. The fish were scared out of their minds because of one thing: a shark! The shark had a very big appetite and loved having visitors for dinner – visitors to eat, of course! The little fish had a major problem. You see, they needed to get to the other side of the shark's territory to find food. They needed to find a way to get to their food and then make it home to shelter before nightfall when the shark would be hungry!

1 Read *A Tale of Little Fish*. Write the **noun groups** for each **noun**.

ocean ______________________

fish ______________________

appetite ______________________

problem ______________________

2 Circle the word in each row that is **not** a **noun**.

fish	shark	eat	dinner
food	shelter	night	swim
think	brain	eye	fin
territory	see	sand	ocean

3 Write a **noun group** of your own to describe each of the following nouns.

______________________ elephant

______________________ dog

______________________ banana

______________________ feet

______________________ kindergarten

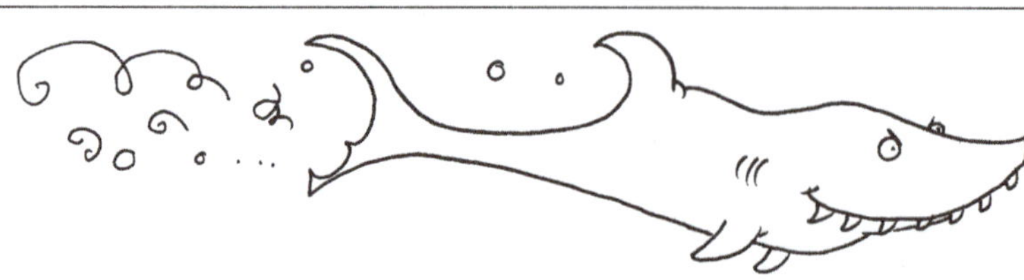

Rule!

Personal pronouns stand for the person speaking.
I me us we
Personal pronouns stand for the person or people being spoken to.
you
Personal pronouns stand for the people or things spoken about.
she her he him it they them

4 Circle the **personal pronoun** used in this sentence.

When you get to the house you will find the key under the doormat.

5 Circle the **personal pronouns** that stand for the baby.

The baby was bored. He crawled around the garden and chewed on his toys. He wanted to play. I took him for a walk around the block in his stroller.

6 Rewrite the sentences replacing each underlined word with a **personal pronoun** from the box.

we	us

My friends and I are going to the bowling alley after school. My friends and I enjoy ten-pin bowling. The owner of the alley lets my friends and I have the same lane each week.

____

____

____

7 Choose a **pronoun** from the box that could represent each **noun** or **noun group**.

she	they	it	it	he

Bill ______________ the boat ______________

Diane ______________ Helen and Kirstin ______________

the house ______________

Try it yourself!

Write the rest of the story *A Tale of Little Fish*. How will the little fish escape the shark and get enough to eat? Use **noun groups** to describe the characters in the story. Use **personal pronouns** to refer to the characters.

Reflection
- I can do this.
- I am not sure.
- I need help.

Unit 6 Revision

1 Underline ten **nouns** for people, places and things in the following sentences.

The children went fishing off the wharf.

Nan and Pop cooked porridge for breakfast.

Bethany rides a bike to school.

I like tadpoles.

2 Underline the **doing verbs**.

I stepped on a thumbtack.

Dad grated the carrots for the salad.

Mum mowed the lawn.

Katy cooked spaghetti.

Melek picked flowers.

3 Change the form of the **doing verbs** in the sentences so that the events happened in the **past**.

The sheep (hop) ____________________ over the log.

We (eat) ____________________ Anzac biscuits.

Mum (buys) ____________________ sausages at the butcher's.

Nonna (walks) ____________________ to the shop.

4 Write a **saying verb** on each line.

Mum ____________________, "Time for bed."

"I'll share with you," ____________________ my little brother.

"Go away!" ____________________ Jessie.

"Where did you put my book?" ____________________ Tam.

Dad ____________________, "Somebody needs to clean the mouse cage."

5 Rewrite each sentence using capital letters for the **proper nouns**.

My aunty likes the music of the band, the beetles.

____

I told andre to come after school on friday.

____

My birthday is in september and emily's birthday is in october.

____

6 Circle the **thinking and feeling verbs**.

I believe she is telling the truth.

I think my cat is the cutest.

The coach worried about the game.

7 Use a **thinking and feeling verb** from the box to complete each sentence.

believed	thought	worried

The little fish ____________________ about the shark.

The little fish ____________________ of a plan.

The shark ____________________ it was the boss of the sea.

8 Join these sentences using a **conjunction** from the box. Write the new sentence on the line.

so	but	because

I walked to the shop. I caught a bus home.

____

It was a beautiful sunny day. We went on a picnic.

____

I was allowed to watch television. I had finished all my homework.

____

9 Write **noun groups** for these things.

a family member ____________________________

a pet ____________________________

a television personality ____________________________

10 Rewrite the paragraph below replacing the underlined words with **personal pronouns**.

My family and I like playing tennis together. <u>My family and I</u> play each Saturday afternoon during the summer. The exercise keeps <u>my family and me</u> fit.

____

____

____

Unit 7

Noun groups, adjectives

These imaginative texts are **poems**. They use **adjectives** in **noun groups** to build up descriptions.

Kakadu Seasons

Wetlands
Steamy air
Vibrant, desperate flowers
Vigorous, pulsing, strident insects
Profusion.

Drylands
Heated air
Rocky, parched landscape
Expectant, haunted, eerie, still
Waiting.

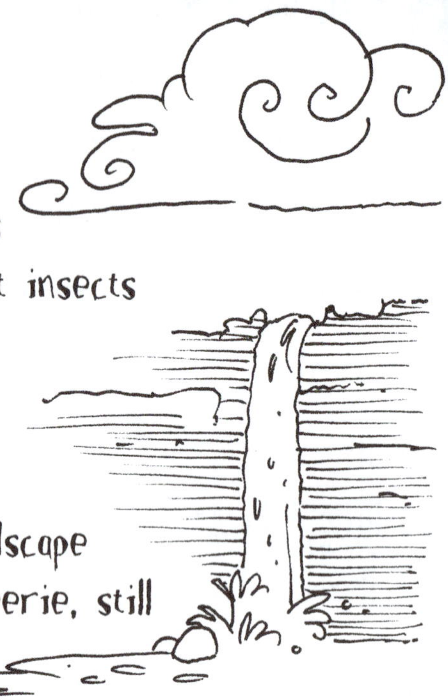

Rule! **Descriptive adjectives** are words that describe a **noun**.

1 Read *Kakadu Seasons*. Write **adjectives** from the poems that describe these **nouns**.

insects ______________________

flowers ______________________

landscape ______________________

air ______________________

2 Underline the **descriptive adjectives** in these **noun groups**.

colourful grasshoppers

hungry dangerous crocodiles

timid little quolls

large grey cranes

3 Write **adjectives** to describe these things. Be as precise as you can.

yourself

____

your school shoes

____

the usual state of your school desk

____

a place in nature

____

4 Complete the table.

Noun	Descriptive adjectives			
	Size	Colour	Shape	Quality
kangaroo			solid	
snake			long	
cloud				
building			angular	
rock				

5 Change the **adjectives** to give each description a different meaning.

The handsome young gentleman stepped out of his battered old car.

___

The fit elderly lady ate her small healthy meal.

___

The energetic little dog waited for her busy owner.

___

6 Write your own **descriptive adjectives**.

________ Suraya tripped over the ________ dog.

________ ________ Desmond walked quietly along the ________ street.

________ Pete drove too fast on the ________ road.

I couldn't wait to read my ________ ________ book.

Sally tried on her ________ ________ riding boots.

Try it yourself!

Kakadu Seasons is made up of two cinquains. A cinquain is a poem with five lines. The structure is one word, two words, three words, four words, one word. Write your own cinquain. Use **adjectives** to precisely describe the **nouns** in your cinquain.

Reflection

- I can do this.
- I am not sure.
- I need help.

Unit 8

Nouns, number adjectives

This informative text is a **recount**. It uses **number adjectives** in the **noun groups**.

Our New Dam

Last June my parents borrowed a neighbour's backhoe. They used it to dig a second dam so our herd of cows would have more water. It took a whole weekend to dig a hole that was deep enough and wide enough, and they had just finished when the rain came. The dam filled very quickly, and after a few weeks a flock of ducks was living in it. We haven't had any rain since then. My mum has used the water in that dam to irrigate our vegetables for the past eight months but the water is nearly all gone now. I hope it rains soon.

1 Read *Our New Dam*. Write nouns from *Our New Dam* that these **adjectives** could describe.

deep, wide ______________________ noisy ______________________

heavy, soaking ______________________ hard-working ______________________

favourite, fresh ______________________ generous, helpful ______________________

2 Circle the **personal pronouns** that refer to the writer in *Our New Dam*.

Rule!

Number adjectives tell you about the quantity or order of a noun.

one *two* *twenty-three* *first* *second* *last*

Some **number adjectives** are **precise**. *five* *second*

Some **number adjectives** are **vague**. *many* *some* *lots* *few*

3 Underline the **number adjectives** in *Our New Dam*. Now write them on the lines.

Precise: ______________ ______________ ______________ Vague: ______________

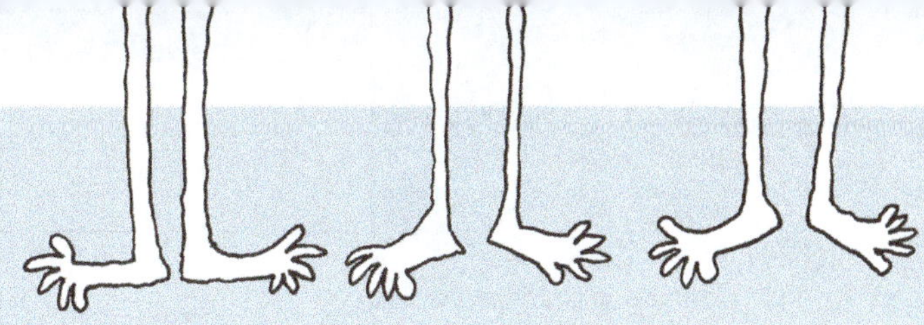

Rule!

A **noun** can be **singular** or **plural**.
singular: *apple* plural: *apples*
A noun can be made **plural** by:
- adding *–s* or *–es* on the end *parent → parents* *peach → peaches*
- changing the spelling in another way *foot → feet* *child → children*

Some nouns don't change at all from singular to plural. *fish* *sheep*

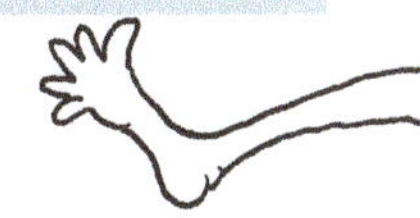

4 Write the **plural** for each **singular noun**. Use a dictionary to check spelling.

half ________________ kangaroo ________________ radius ________________

child ________________ woman ________________ baby ________________

Rule!

Collective nouns are names for groups of things. **Collective nouns** are **singular** even though they refer to a number of things in their group because there is one group.

flock *herd* *bunch* *gang*

5 There are two **collective nouns** in *Our New Dam*. Write them on the lines.

________________ ________________

6 Choose a **collective noun** from the box for each group.

pod	string	bouquet	team	fleet	pride

a ________________ of whales a ________________ of lions

a ________________ of footballers a ________________ of ships

a ________________ of pearls a ________________ of flowers

7 Work with a partner to create a sentence for each **collective noun** in the box.

choir	gaggle	army	litter	clutch	crew

Try it yourself!

Use a dictionary to find some **plural** and **singular** nouns. Find ten for each category: ends in *–s*, ends in *–es*, other spelling change, no spelling change. Compare your lists with a partner's lists.

Reflection

- I can do this.
- I am not sure.
- I need help.

Unit 9

Possessive pronouns, possessive adjectives

This informative text is a **recount**. It uses **possessive pronouns** and **possessive adjectives** to signal who owns what.

Dear Mum,

I'm having a great time at Nan's and Pop's farm. Last month, Lilly had a litter. Pop kept one of the puppies. Her name is Lulu. Yesterday I did some chores. First I cleaned out the chicken coop. The chickens were friendly, but their coop was smelly. I also cleaned the dogs' kennel. The dogs got excited when I went near their kennel because they thought I was going to give them their dinner. Pop's chores are much harder than mine. Yesterday he had to fix some fences. I have to go now. Pop and I are going to town for our lunch today.

Miss you.

Love,
Skye

Rule!

Possessive pronouns show ownership.

his hers theirs yours mine ours

The hat is his. *The farm is theirs.* *The book is mine.*

1 Complete each sentence with a **possessive pronoun** from the box.

his	hers	theirs	yours	mine	ours

Adam says that the CD is ______________.

They told me that car was ______________.

Give that back to Shelly, it's ______________!

Take the prize. You won it, it's ______________.

It's my job to feed the fish, because they are ______________.

That house is ______________!

2 Read *Dear Mum*. Circle the **possessive pronoun**. Hint! There is only one.

Rule!

Nouns and **noun groups** can include words that show ownership. These are **possessive adjectives**.

Our old dog his her their your my our its

3 In *Dear Mum*, underline the **possessive adjectives** that show ownership. Hint! There are five.

4 Use a **possessive adjective** from the box to complete each sentence.

their	his	her	its

__________ boots are dirty. (Pop's boots

I like __________ name. (Lulu's name)

__________ farm is fun. (Nan's and Pop's farm)

I gave the cow __________ water. (the cow's water)

Rule!

An **apostrophe** can show ownership. An apostrophe with a noun shows that something belongs to that noun.

singular noun	add 's	*Jim's dog*
plural noun ending in s	add '	*the ducks' pond*
plural noun not ending in s	add 's	*the children's cubby house*

5 Rewrite each sentence using an **apostrophe**.
That is the coop belonging to the chickens. = That is the chickens' coop.

Those are the shoes belonging to the twins. = __________

Where is the dog that belongs to Amiri? = __________

The presents belonging to the children are here! = __________

That is the desk belonging to the teacher. = __________

Those are the yachts belonging to the sailors. = __________

Try it yourself!

Write a **recount** that includes some information on things that belong to people. Use **possessive pronouns**, **possessive adjectives** and **apostrophes** to show who owns what.

Reflection

- I can do this.
- I am not sure.
- I need help.

Unit 10

Simple sentences, relating verbs

This informative text is an **information report**. It uses **relating verbs** to show relationships.

Australia's Mightiest River System

Australia's longest river is the Murray. It is 2520 kilometres long. It travels through New South Wales and South Australia. Australia's longest river system is the Murray–Darling, which starts in Queensland as the Darling River and ends in South Australia where the Murray River flows into the sea. The Murray–Darling system is 3370 kilometres long. In 2007 the Murray–Darling was listed by the World Wide Fund for Nature (WWF) as one of the world's top ten rivers at risk from problems caused by pollution, climate change, dams and introduced fish and plants.

Rule!

Relating verbs show relationships, such as being and having. You cannot see any action taking place.

is belongs equals was had are

1 Read *Australia's Mightiest River System*. Then circle the **relating verbs** in the following statements.

The river is 2520 kilometres long.

The river has a number of problems.

The river was at risk.

The river belongs to a system of waterways.

2 Choose a **relating verb** from the box to complete each sentence.

is	belongs	equals	was	had	are

Two plus two ____________ four.

My favourite food ____________ lasagne but now I prefer spaghetti.

It ____________ lunchtime.

You ____________ my best friend.

The lunch box ____________ to Bintang.

Jodie ____________ a photo of a bunyip.

Rule! A **sentence** is a group of words that makes sense on its own. It must include at least one **verb**.

3 Circle the **verbs** in the **sentences** below.

The WWF conducts surveys.

Rivers are powerful.

The crocodile had a delicious lunch.

The canoe crashed over the waterfall.

I thought the pirate was ugly.

4 Unjumble these words to write **sentences** from *Australia's Mightiest River System*. Use correct punctuation.

is 2520 long kilometres it ______________________________

travels through it new south wales and south australia

____

longest river the murray is australia's ______________________________

5 Tick the word groups that are **sentences**. Remember, a sentence must include a **verb**.

A fat toad.

Along the way.

Water flows.

I eat sea slugs.

Freya and Wilma said no.

6 Add some words to make complete sentences. Remember, sentences must make sense.

For five days now ______________________________.

Ron and Ingrid took turns to ______________________________.

Last holidays ______________________________.

Many people prefer ______________________________.

Crocodiles are ______________________________.

Try it yourself!

Use the internet. Do some research on a place in Australia. Create an **information report**. Add images and create a short slide show to present the information to the class.

Reflection

- I can do this.
- I am not sure.
- I need help.

Unit 11

Questions and statements, clauses

The Driest Place on Earth

Antarctica is approximately twice the size of Australia. Seventy per cent of the world's fresh water is frozen in Antarctica. Even though it holds more water than all the other continents combined, Antarctica is the driest continent on earth. It is called a frozen desert. Antarctica is also the windiest continent on earth with hurricane-force winds reaching up to 250 kilometres per hour. The coldest temperature ever recorded, –89.6°C, also belongs to Antarctica. After Antarctica, Australia is the next driest continent on earth.

This informative text is an **information report**. It gives information in factual **statements**.

Rule!

A **statement** gives information or an opinion. It ends in a full stop.

Penguins live in Antartica. *I think penguins are cute.*

A **question** asks for information or an opinion. It ends in a question mark.

What is the time? *Do you think you'll finish your homework?*

1 Read *The Driest Place on Earth*. Find four **statements** of fact. Write a **question** for each one.

Question: How big is Antarctica compared to Australia?

Answer: Antarctica is approximately twice the size of Australia.

Question: ______________________________

Answer: ______________________________

Question: ______________________________

Answer: ______________________________

Question: ______________________________

Answer: ______________________________

Question: ______________________________

Answer: ______________________________

2 Write **statement** or **question** after each sentence. Then finish each sentence with the correct punctuation marker.

When will we eat dinner ________________ Where are my keys ________________

We'll eat dinner at 6 pm ________________ Did you phone Uncle Van ____________

I'll set the dinner table for six people ____________

3 Write a **question** beginning with each word. Remember to use a question mark at the end.

Who ____

What ____

When ____

Where ____

Why ____

How ____

Rule!

A **clause** is a group of words that expresses an idea and contains a **verb**. A **sentence** can be made up of just one clause or a number of clauses.

Conjunctions are joining words. They link clauses in a sentence.

and *so* *because*

4 Choose a **conjunction** from the box to join each pair of clauses.

because	so	and

Antarctica is called a frozen desert. It is so dry.

____

Antarctica is windy. Antarctica is cold.

____

The old television doesn't work. We need to buy a new one.

____

Try it yourself!

Choose a topic that interests you. Write some **questions** that you have about the topic. Research your topic and write an **information report** that provides **statements** of information to answer your questions. Create a short slide show to present the information to the class.

Reflection

- I can do this.
- I am not sure.
- I need help.

Unit 12 Revision

1 Write **noun groups**. Use a **number adjective** and another **adjective** to precisely describe the following nouns. Write the **number adjective** first.

______________________________ crabs

______________________________ dolphins

______________________________ shark

______________________________ mermaids

2 Choose a word from the box for each **noun group** to show ownership.

our	its	my	his

My hat blew away and __________ brim got torn.

"Has someone taken __________ hat?" asked Katy.

He liked staying at __________ uncle's place.

__________ school won the swimming carnival.

3 Rewrite these word groups using an **apostrophe** to show possession.

The groceries belonging to the shoppers = ______________________________

The tea belonging to Mum = ______________________________

The dog belonging to Aunty Laura = ______________________________

The cars belonging to the teachers = ______________________________

The books belonging to the library = ______________________________

4 Circle the **relating verbs**.

My mother is a deep-sea diver.

My parents are swimmers.

My great-grandmother was Japanese.

This book belongs on my desk.

5 Cross out the word groups that are not **sentences**.

I like to go to the.

Too many sharks.

Kate fed her dog.

By the way.

Do you have a pencil?

6 Unjumble the words and write the sentences on the lines. Use correct punctuation.

school to day children walk each many

____

cover when sneeze mouth your you

____

the our visit during we will holidays school grandfather

____

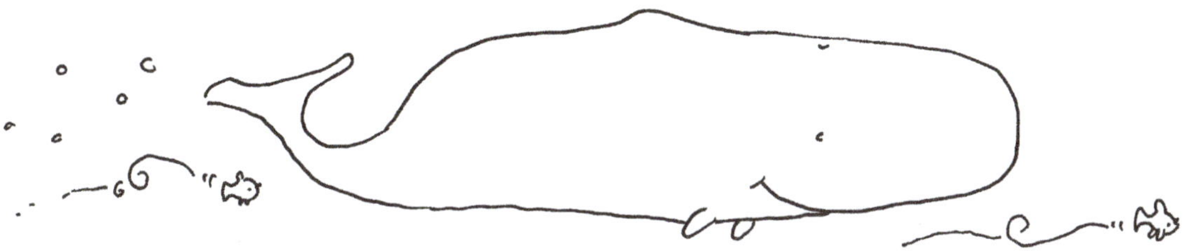

7 Choose a **possessive pronoun** from the box to complete each sentence and show ownership.

his	hers	theirs	yours	mine	ours

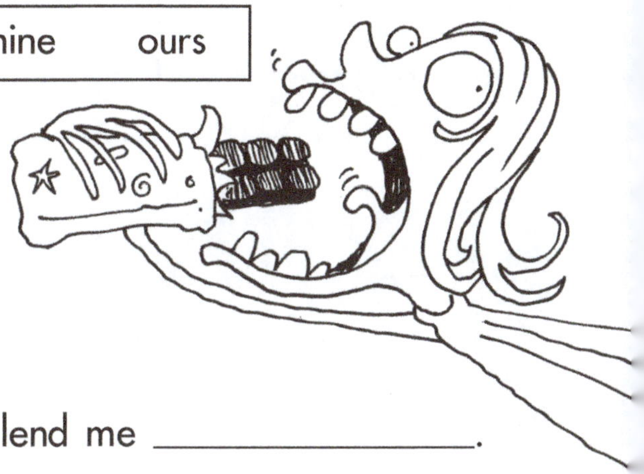

My name's Hakim, what's ______________?

Hands off that chocolate, it's ______________!

I'm sure the white jacket is ______________.

Josh admitted the mess was ______________.

I won't take a surfboard because Sadie and Liam will lend me ______________.

They already have tickets, so let's go and buy ______________.

8 Draw lines to show which **clauses** go together to make a **sentence**.

I'll clean my room	**but** she's still hungry.
I would like sprinkles	**because** he hasn't been fed yet.
I can play	**because** I have finished my homework.
The dog is hungry	**so** you can sleep over.
The cat has been fed	**and** topping on my ice-cream.

Unit 13 Prepositions, prepositional phrases

Under the Sea

This imaginative text is an illustration for a **narrative**. Things in the illustration can be located using **prepositional phrases**.

Rule! A **preposition** is a word that shows the relationship between a **noun** or **pronoun** and another word.

They can tell <u>where</u>. *in on under over beside off*

They can tell <u>when</u>. *during after before*

1 Circle the **preposition** in each statement about the *Under the Sea* illustration.

There is an oyster in the water.

A pearl is inside the oyster.

A crab is beside the oyster.

Bubbles are coming from the scuba diver.

A seahorse floats near some seaweed.

Rule! A **prepositional phrase** is a preposition linked to a noun or noun group.

near the stove *under the bed* *in the kitchen cupboard*

2 Underline the **prepositions** in each **prepositional phrase**. Then draw each new thing on *Under the Sea*.

A sea slug on the rock

A treasure chest on the ground

A fish with the crab

A trident beside the mermaid

Some shells near the rock

A dolphin above the seaweed

3 Circle the **prepositions**. Underline the **prepositional phrases**.

I had a snack during the night.

Slide the letter under the door.

The cow jumped over the moon.

Tip! **Homonyms** are words that sound the same but are spelled differently and have different meanings.

their *Their tails are curly.*
there *The oyster is there.*
they're *They're looking at the mermaid.*
Notice the apostrophe in *they're*.

4 Write *there, their* or *they're* on the lines.

Ted borrowed ______________ lawnmower.

My neighbours want ______________ lawnmower back.

Ted said he already left it ______________.

______________ going to be angry if ______________ lawnmower is lost.

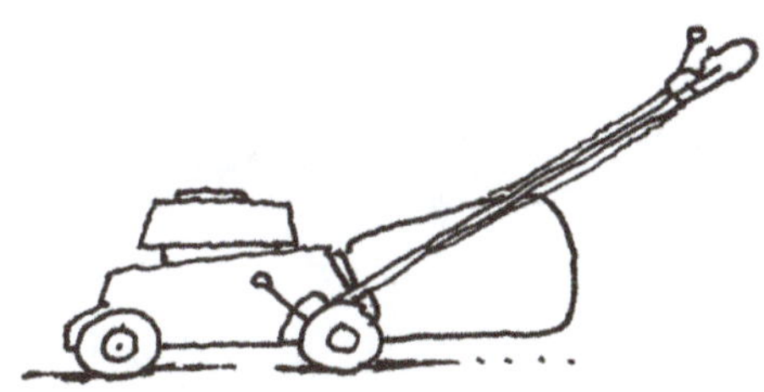

5 **Prepositions** can tell where. Write sentences with **prepositional phrases** to describe the position of two things that you can see in your classroom.

The book is on the teacher's desk.

____

____

Try it yourself!

Write a narrative to match the *Under the Sea* illustration. Use **noun groups** to describe the characters and **prepositional phrases** to tell where things are.

Reflection

- I can do this.
- I am not sure.
- I need help.

Unit 14

Doing verbs, prepositional phrases

This informative text is a **procedure** in the form of a recipe. It uses **verbs** to tell what to do.

Frog Potion

How to turn a frog into a handsome prince

Ingredients

- 1 strand of a prince's hair
- 1 hair off the back of the troll that lives under the bridge
- 1 tablespoon of ogre's swamp
- 1 scale from a mermaid's tail
- 1 dragon's tooth
- 1 pinch of sand from the bottom of the ocean

Method

1. Mix ingredients together to make the potion.
2. Make the frog swallow the potion.
3. Close your eyes.
4. Chant three times to the frog:
   You are now a handsome prince.

1 Read the *Frog Potion* recipe. Underline each **prepositional phrase**. Hint! Look for these prepositions: *of, off, under, from*.

2 Write four **doing verbs** used in the Method of the recipe.

____

3 Write ingredients that include **prepositional phrases** for a recipe of your own.

How to ______________________________

____

____

____

____

Tip! Recipes require people to take action. That's why most steps in the recipe start with a **doing verb**.

4 Circle the **verbs** in the box that you might find in a normal recipe.

stir	type	bake	spit	throw	argue	yell	cook	blend	tell	fry

5 Create a Method for a crazy recipe. Write four steps in the Method. Start each step with one of the verbs that you did not circle in question 4.

____

____

____

____

Rule! A **command** is a sentence that tells someone to do something. It often begins with a **verb**.

6 Edit the text so that it is a numbered set of **commands** for a recipe.

Please mix together the flour and the butter and the sugar, if you like. Please be careful not to hurt yourself. If you spill any flour you might like to wipe it up so you don't make a mess. If you are tired you could have a rest and watch some television for a while. I don't know. Maybe you won't like these biscuits. You could probably add the sultanas and coconut now. Then you have to make little balls of the dough and put them on an oven tray and bake them for about 35 minutes. I hope that's OK. Did you like them?

Try it yourself!

Create a recipe of your own. Use **noun groups** for the ingredients. Ask a peer to help edit your work.

Reflection

- I can do this.
- I am not sure.
- I need help.

How to Catch a Fish

1. Get some plastic lures to use for bait.
2. Attach a lure to the hook on your fishing line.
3. Dangle the baited hook in the water.
4. Sit quietly and patiently.
5. Pull swiftly on the line when you feel a fish take the hook.
6. Bring in the fish, keeping tension on the line.
7. Keep the fish for dinner, if it is of legal size.
8. Release the fish if you do not intend to eat it.

This informative text is a **procedure** that gives instructions. Each step is a **command**. **Adverbs** tell how to do things.

1 Read *How to Catch a Fish*. Write the **doing verb** that begins each command.

____

____

2 Write a **command** that the fish could give to the person who has caught it.

____

Rule! Some **adverbs** add meaning to verbs by telling <u>how</u>.

slowly *suddenly* *angrily* *busily* *carefully*

3 Find three **adverbs** in *How to Catch a Fish* that tell <u>how</u>.

____

4 Choose an **adverb** from the box to complete each **command**.

quickly	bravely	sweetly	slowly	carefully

Walk ________________ because we are running late.

Tread ________________ on the slippery rocks.

Eat ________________ or you'll get indigestion.

Sing ________________ so you'll be picked for the concert.

Smile ________________ for the photo.

5 Add an **adverb** to each instruction.

________________ attach the bait to a hook on your line.

________________ dangle the baited hook in the water.

Release the fish ________________ if you do not intend to eat it.

6 Replace the underlined words with an **adverb** that tells how. Rewrite the sentences.

Eat <u>in a slow way</u> = Eat <u>slowly</u>.

Cross <u>at a brisk pace</u> = ________________________________

The children played <u>in a happy manner</u> = ________________________

The dolphin jumped <u>with ease</u> over the boat = ____________________

____

Try it yourself!

Write a set of instructions for catching something: a cold, a snake, an egg, a possum, or anything else you can think of. Start each step with a **doing verb**. Use **adverbs** to add meaning to the verbs.

Reflection

- I can do this.
- I am not sure.
- I need help.

Unit 16

Noun groups, verb tense

This informative text is a **procedure** that provides instructions. The **verbs** are written in the **present timeless tense.**

Sun Safety

- Slip on a dark-coloured sun shirt with long sleeves.
- Slop on some SPF 30+ sunscreen and reapply every two hours.
- Slap on a wide-brimmed, legionnaire or bucket-style sunhat.
- Slide on some Cancer Council Australia recommended sunglasses.
- Seek out some shade and avoid the sun between 10 am and 3 pm.

Tip!

A **noun group** can contain more than one noun.
The extra noun or nouns tell more about the **main noun.**
Look at the catfish that has crossed eyes.

1 Read *Sun Safety* and underline the **noun groups**. Circle the main **noun** in each group.

2 Circle the main **noun** in each **noun group**. Then write a sentence using the **noun group**.

the old run-down house across the street

____

the photo of Diego when he was a nipper

____

Gemma's friend Rowan

____

3 Add a **noun group** to complete each sentence. Circle each main **noun**.

The ____________________________ swam away with the ball.

The ____________________________ ate all the seaweed.

We all looked for the ____________________________ .

Rule! **Verbs** can show whether an action happened in the past, is happening now, happens always or has not yet happened. This is called the **tense**.

past tense	*she went*	
present tense	*she goes*	*she is going*
future tense	*she will go*	

4 Change the **verb** form so that the events happened in the **past**.

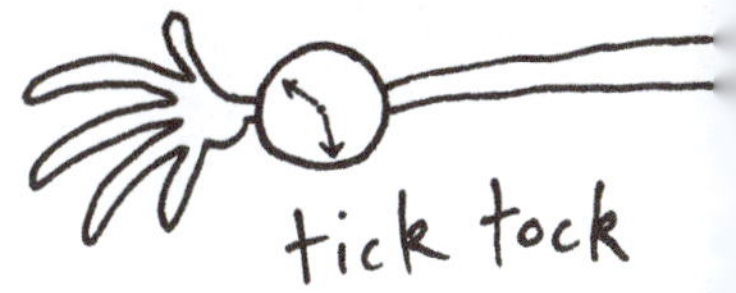

Present timeless tense	Past tense
She eats salad for lunch.	______________
Tibby jumps on the bed.	______________
Gran drives to work.	______________
Dad listens to music.	______________
My dog slips on tiles.	______________

5 Change the **verbs** to **past tense**. Then use the past tense verbs to complete the sentences.

slip ____________ slop ____________ go ____________

slap ____________ slide ____________

When I ____________ to the beach I ____________ on a shirt, ____________ on some sunscreen and ____________ on a hat. I also ____________ on some sunglasses.

Try it yourself!

Write a set of **rules** for your home. You can make the rules serious or funny. Write in the **present tense**. Use extended **noun groups** if they are useful to clarify the meaning of your rules.

Reflection

- I can do this.
- I am not sure.
- I need help.

Unit 17

Commands, doing verbs, proper nouns

This informative text is a **procedure** that gives instructions. It uses **commands** beginning with **verbs** to tell what to do.

Directions to the Olympic Pool

From my house it is 1.5 kilometres to the Olympic swimming pool. These are the directions to get to the pool from my home:

1. Turn right out of my front gate.
2. Walk to the corner of the next street, which is Olsen Avenue.
3. Cross Olsen Avenue at the traffic lights.
4. Turn left into Olsen Avenue and walk two blocks until you come to the pedestrian crossing on Smith Street.
5. Cross Smith Street and turn right.
6. Walk one block to Charles Road.
7. Cross Charles Road at the pedestrian crossing and you will have arrived at the pool.

Tip! The clearest way to write directions is to use **commands** and include **doing verbs**.

1 Circle the **doing verbs** in *Directions to the Olympic Pool*.

2 Choose a **doing verb** from the box to begin each **command**. Remember to begin the sentence with a capital letter.

walk	swim	catch	crawl	fly

_______________ across the road.

_______________ in a seaplane.

_______________ the bus.

_______________ around the island.

_______________ through the tunnel.

3 Underline the **proper nouns** in *Directions to the Olympic Pool*.

Grammar Rules!

______________________'s Writing Log

1 Think

What is your topic?
What is the purpose of the writing?
Who is the audience?
What type of text and text form will you use?

2 Draft

Gather your ideas.
Organise your ideas.
Have a go at writing.

3 Revise

Check your writing for meaning and ideas.
- *Have you chosen the best words and phrases for your topic?*
- *Do you need to add anything?*
- *Do you need to take anything away?*
- *Do you need to move anything?*

Check your writing for structure.
- *Does the structure match the type of text you chose?*

Read your writing to a partner.
Read your writing to your teacher.
Ask for help to improve your writing.

4 Proofread

Polish your writing.
Check your grammar.
Check your spelling.
Check your punctuation.

5 Publish

Publish your writing.
Share your writing.
Reflect on your writing.

Create symbols for a rating scale. Then each time you finish a piece of writing, record it in the log.

My rating scale

Symbol	Meaning
	Help!
	A good start.
	I have the basics covered.
	I'm beyond the basics.
	Brilliant!

Do you need some ideas for other text forms to try? Look at the back page!

Date	Title	Type of text and text form	Audienc
Write the date.	Write the title of your piece.	eg recount/ letter	Who were you writing <u>for</u> or

Grammar I used	My rating	Where to next?
t the main grammar features you used.	Record your rating.	What grammar could you try next? How could you improve your writing? Does your teacher have any comments?

I've tried these types of texts and text forms . . .

Narrative (imaginative)

- [ ] Story
- [ ] Comic
- [ ] Other ____________________

Recount (imaginative or informative)

- [ ] Letter
- [ ] Newspaper article
- [ ] Other ____________________

Description (imaginative or informative)

- [ ] Poem
- [ ] Police report
- [ ] Letter
- [ ] Story
- [ ] Other ____________________

Information report (informative)

- [ ] Scientific report
- [ ] Website
- [ ] Other ____________________

Procedure (informative)

- [ ] Cookbook
- [ ] Instruction manual
- [ ] Game rules
- [ ] Other ____________________

Explanation (informative)

- [ ] Reference book
- [ ] Other ____________________

Exposition (persuasive) (argues one side of an issue)

- [ ] Debate
- [ ] Speech
- [ ] Letter to editor
- [ ] TV advertisement
- [ ] Magazine advertisement
- [ ] Leaflet
- [ ] Other ____________________

Discussion (persuasive) (presents more than one side of an issue)

- [ ] Conversation
- [ ] TV interview
- [ ] Talk-back radio
- [ ] Dialogue in a story
- [ ] Panel discussion
- [ ] Other ____________________

Response (persuasive)

- [ ] Diary
- [ ] Book review
- [ ] Poem
- [ ] Other ____________________

4 Complete each **command** with a **proper noun** from the box.

Aunty Freda	Dimitri	Dingle Street	Watson's	Tiggles

Say hello to ____________________.

Deliver the letter to ____________________.

Wash ____________________.

Invite your friend ____________________ to your party.

Buy bread at ____________________ supermarket.

5 Rewrite the **statements** using capital letters for the **proper nouns**. Remember that a statement starts with a capital letter and ends with a full stop.

the letter is addressed to robyn nguyen at 29 alfred street, pentiville

____

uncle hien lives in ascot, which is a suburb of brisbane

____

cradle mountain is a beautiful area in tasmania

____

frozen world ice rink is on boona street in forestville

____

6 Write a set of directions to get from your classroom to your school principal's office. Number each step. Use **doing verbs**.

____

____

____

____

____

Try it yourself!

Write a set of directions. Use your home as a starting point. Make sure you write the directions in logical order and use **doing verbs**. Remember that **proper nouns** (for street names, suburbs, towns and venues) have capital letters.

Reflection

- I can do this.
- I am not sure.
- I need help.

Unit 18 Revision

1 Underline the **prepositional phrases** in each sentence. Circle the **prepositions**.

Jacob threw three coins in the fountain.

I dropped a shell on the floor.

My neighbour stood at the window.

The street was flooded after the storm.

A bridge swung over the river.

2 Write sentences with **prepositional phrases** to describe the location of three things in your home.

____

____

____

3 Change the **verb** form so that the events happened in the **past**.

Present tense	Past tense
Ivan is hurrying his homework.	______________
Sunita is running quickly.	______________
The leopard seal is chasing the penguin.	______________
Christopher is outside.	______________
Grandma is enjoying her book.	______________

4 Choose an **adverb** from the box to complete each sentence.

noisily	greedily	frantically	mistakenly

I ______________ took the wrong fish home.

The dog ______________ devoured its dinner.

My sister slurped her ice-cream ______________.

Mum ______________ searched for her purse.

5 Write five **doing verbs** that you would find in a recipe.

____

6 Write two rules that apply in your classroom. Write each rule as a **command** beginning with a **doing verb**.

____

____

7 Rewrite each sentence. Replace the underlined words with an **adverb** that tells how.

Cross the road in a careful manner. ______________________

The children played in a noisy manner. ______________________

The horse jumped in a clumsy manner over the fence.

____

Mum sang in a loud manner. ______________________

8 Write a **noun group** for the underlined noun in each sentence.

The Wilsons live in the ______________________ submarine.

The ______________________ children entered the competition.

The ______________________ photo was rumpled.

I saw the ______________________ penguin.

9 Rewrite the **statements** correctly. Remember that a **statement** starts with a capital letter and ends with a full stop, and **proper nouns** begin with a capital letter.

santa clause lives at the north pole ______________________

my teacher's name is ms hickman ______________________

debbie and lucy went together to frankie's house on shark island

____

the dog's collar stated its address as 101 hill street, fairlight

____

king neptune child care centre is on trident street

____

Unit 19 Quoted and reported speech

This imaginative text is a comic strip **narrative**. It uses speech balloons instead of **speech marks** to quote what the characters are saying.

Rule!

Quoted speech (direct speech) is the actual speech someone says. It is written inside **speech marks**.

"Can I splash?" asked Maya. "Yes," said Mum.

1 Put the **speech marks** in the correct places.

I love you, said Dad.

Where are you? called Louella.

Go away! shouted Bindi.

How many apples will I get? asked Teresa.

Eddie, please sit quietly at your desk, said the teacher.

2 Record the speech in *Super Crab* as **quoted speech** with **speech marks**.

____

____

____

____

____

Rule! **Reported speech** (indirect speech) is speech that is not quoted directly.
Maya asked if she could splash.

3 Change the **quoted speech** in question 1 to **reported speech**.

4 Write speech inside each balloon to show what the characters are saying.

5 Write a conversation between two people. Use **quoted speech**.

Try it yourself!

Create a comic strip of your own that uses speech balloons to quote the **quoted speech**. Ask a peer to comment on your comic strip.

Reflection

- I can do this.
- I am not sure.
- I need help.

Unit 20 Theme

Isabel Letham, Surfie Legend

This informative text is a **recount** in the form of a biography. It retells important events in a person's life. The person's name is used in **theme** position in a number of clauses.

The first Australian to ride a surfboard was a woman named Isabel Letham. Isabel was fifteen when legendary Hawaiian surfer Duke Kahanamoku visited Australia and rode his surfboard in a surfing exhibition at Freshwater Beach. Isabel was on the beach watching the exhibition when Duke, also known as 'The Big Kahuna', asked for a volunteer to ride tandem with him. Isabel was chosen and became an instant celebrity in Australia and overseas. Isabel was involved in water sports all her life. She died in 1995 at age 96.

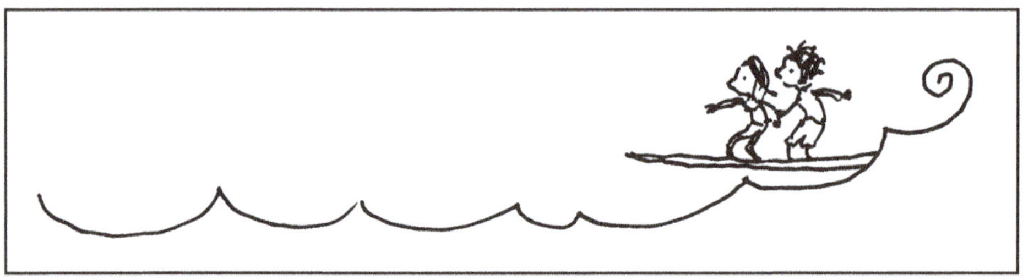

Rule!

Theme is the first part of a clause. It tells what a sentence is about. Theme helps to connect information across a text.

The first Australian to ride a surfboard was a woman.
theme

1 Read *Isabel Letham, Surfie Legend.* There are six sentences. Underline the **theme** at the beginning of each sentence.

2 Underline the **theme** in each sentence.

Australia is famous for its surfing beaches.

The surf life saving movement started in 1907.

Surf Life Saving Australia celebrated its 100th anniversary in 2007.

Swimmers must look out for rips.

3 Write sentences using each **noun group** in the box in **theme** position.

Mum and Jerry	The little black dog	The beach	An apple

Tip! Sometimes words other than nouns and noun groups are used in **theme** position to highlight their importance to the meaning of a text.

4 Underline the **theme** of each **statement**.

In Sydney the Harbour Bridge is a famous tourist attraction.

On Tuesdays we have soccer practice.

Eating fruit and vegetables is recommended to maintain good health.

Occasionally we fish from the dock.

5 Underline the theme of each **command**.

Practise piano every day.

Apply sunscreen liberally.

Swim between the flags.

6 Underline the **theme** in each clause.

Rips are strong currents. They are stronger when the surf is bigger. They run out to sea. A tired swimmer can easily get caught in a rip. The worst thing you can do is panic.

Try it yourself!

Write a biography of someone you know. Interview the person to get the facts of their life. Write the facts in the order that they happened. Use **noun groups** or **pronouns** that represent your topic in **theme** position in each sentence.

Reflection

- I can do this.
- I am not sure.
- I need help.

Theme; statements (declarative mood); commands (imperative mood)

Unit **21** Helping verbs, verb tense

Recycled Water

There is a fixed amount of water on earth. It all developed about four billion years ago and since that time has been recycled many millions of times in what is called the water cycle. In the water cycle, water evaporates from the oceans and rivers into the air. This evaporated water condenses into fog and mist, and forms clouds. The clouds move to the mountains and release water as rain, hail and snow. This water then forms rivers that flow to the ocean. Then the cycle begins again.

1 Read *Recycled Water*. Circle the **verbs** or **verb groups** below that are used in *Recycled Water*.

is *developed* *is called* *evaporates* *dreams*
condenses *jumped* *move* *release* *joins*
forms *dancing* *flow* *begins* *has been recycled*

Rule!

A **verb group** contains a main verb and verbs that 'help' it.
is called
has been recycled
Helping verbs can show the tense.
future tense: *will be recycled*
past tense: *was recycled*

2 Underline the **verb group** in each sentence. Circle the **helping verbs**.

The water has been recycled.
It was developed a long time ago.
It is called the water cycle.
Water has been carried in clouds.
The clouds have moved to the mountains.

3 Use a **helping verb** from the box to complete each sentence. Then tick the **present** or **past** column after each one.

are	had	have	is	was	were

	Present	Past
The dog __________ moved the bone.		
We __________ eaten breakfast.		
We __________ making dinner.		
Margo __________ going out.		
Jana __________ yelling.		
Brett and I __________ running to the bus stop.		

4 Insert a **helping verb** to show that these actions will happen in the future.

We ______________ go to soccer practice later on.

Ozan ______________ have pizza for dinner.

The teacher ______________ mark the homework.

5 Change the **verb** form to show that these actions happened in the **past**.

We (walk) ________________ to school yesterday.

A frog (hop) ________________ past our door.

Mayumi (run) ________________ home.

Joseph (eat) ________________ quickly.

Ken (borrow) ________________ the book.

Try it yourself!

Write an **explanation** for a subject related to something you are doing in class. Use **present tense** for your **verb groups**. Ask a peer to help edit your work.

Reflection

- I can do this.
- I am not sure.
- I need help.

Unit 22

Theme, personal pronouns, possessive adjectives

This persuasive text is an **exposition** in the form of an advertisement. It uses **commands** with **doing verbs** in **theme** position to persuade people to take action.

We Tank You

RAINWATER TANKS

Install a rainwater tank.

Collect your own rainwater.

Beat water restrictions.

Help the environment.

Reduce your water bills – rainwater is free!

Call now on 1309 999 99 to arrange a free quote.

WE TANK YOU BECAUSE WE CARE

1 Read *We Tank You*. Circle the **doing verbs** used in **theme** position.

2 Write a synonym for each **theme** position **doing verb** in *We Tank You*. Make sure the advertisement still makes sense.

______________ your own rainwater.

______________ a rainwater tank.

______________ water restrictions.

______________ now on 1309 999 99.

______________ your water bills.

______________ the environment.

3 Write a **verb** from the box in the **theme** position in each sentence.

cross	jump	eat	look	sit

______________ your vegetables.

______________ the road carefully.

______________ up straight.

______________ over the puddle.

______________ at the octopus.

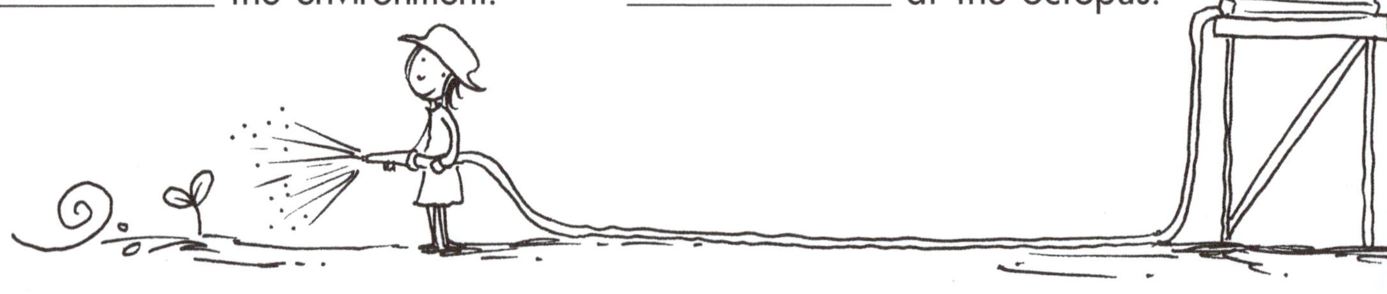

Tip! Advertisers sometimes use **personal pronouns** (*I me we us you*) and **possessive adjectives** (*your our*) to make their advertisements seem more personal.

4 Write a **statement** after each **command** to state that you will obey.

Install a rainwater tank. <u>I will install a rainwater tank</u>.

Collect your own rainwater. ____________________

Beat restrictions. ____________________

Help the environment. ____________________

Reduce your water bills. ____________________

Call now on 1309 999 99. ____________________

5 Complete each command to tell customers about other features of, or uses for, the rainwater tanks. Be as crazy as you like.

Use your tank for ____________________

Hope your tank is ____________________

Hug ____________________

Catch ____________________

____

6 Choose a **pronoun** from the box to complete each sentence.

I	me	we
you	us	

________ ate my fish first.

________ had seaweed for dinner.

Mum gave ________ a fish tank.

Did ________ find a crocodile?

Dad gave ________ a surfboard.

Try it yourself!

Write an advertisement to persuade your classmates to buy a classroom item such as a pen, a book, or a chair. Use **commands** with **doing verbs** in **theme** position.

Reflection

- I can do this.
- I am not sure.
- I need help.

Unit 23 Conjunctions, comparative adjectives

This informative text is an **information report**. It uses **comparative adjectives** to describe the topic. It uses **conjunctions** to join clauses.

Lake Eyre

The largest lake in Australia, when it is filled with water, is Lake Eyre in South Australia. Lake Eyre spreads over 9500 square kilometres. It can be 6 metres deep at its deepest part; however, it is usually just a dry salt pan. In some parts the salt layers are up to 50 centimetres thick. Lake Eyre only filled with water three times in the hundred years between 1900 and 2000. Mostly it looks like a shining, sparkling sheet of white salt.

The Lake Eyre dragon is a tiny lizard that has evolved to survive in this harsh, salty habitat. It walks on the heels of its feet, with its toes off the ground so it doesn't get burnt feet.

1 Read *Lake Eyre*. Circle *it* and *its* in blue pencil when they refer to Lake Eyre. Circle *it* and *its* in red pencil when they refer to the Lake Eyre dragon.

2 Underline the words in each pair of sentences that could be replaced with *it*.

Lake Eyre is in South Australia. Lake Eyre is a salt lake.

The Lake Eyre dragon is a lizard. The Lake Eyre dragon does not like to have hot toes.

The Lake Eyre dragon is a reptile. The Lake Eyre dragon eats ants and tiny insects.

Rule!

Conjunctions are joining words. They can link clauses in a sentence by:

- adding information — *and*
- comparing things — *however* *but* *or*
- showing one thing causes another — *so* *because*
- showing a time sequence — *when* *then*

3 Find the **conjunctions** in *Lake Eyre*. Write them on the line.

____

4 Use **conjunctions** to join each pair of sentences.

Lake Eyre dragons have sharp claws. The females can dig holes to lay their eggs.

____

Lake Eyre dragons have sharp claws. They cannot hurt people.

____

Lake Eyre dragons live on Lake Eyre. Pebble dragons live on Lake Eyre.

____

Rule!

Comparative and **superlative adjectives** can be used to compare things.

long → longer → longest

frightening → more frightening → most frightening

5 Find the **comparative adjectives** in *Lake Eyre*. Hint! There are two.

____________________ ____________________

6 Complete the table.

Adjective	Comparative	Superlative
deep	deeper	deepest
big		
small		
slow		
funny		

7 Some adjectives use the words *more* and *most* to make their **comparative** and **superlative** forms. Write *more* or *most* on the lines.

The surgeon was ______________ clever than his colleague.

The surgeon was the ______________ clever surgeon in the hospital.

The athlete was the ______________ energetic on her team.

Try it yourself!

Search the internet to find appropriate material to create an **information report** on a topic you are studying in class. Collect and insert a number of images and create a short slide show to present the information to the class.

Reflection

- I can do this.
- I am not sure.
- I need help.

Unit 24 Revision

1 Put **speech marks** in the correct places to show **quoted speech** (direct speech).

Put it in the oven now, said Dad.

Where are you going? asked Tahlee.

Stop! shouted Roberto.

How is your new goldfish? asked Zac.

The pirate announced, Be careful on the gangplank.

2 Circle the **theme** of each sentence.

Liesl Jones is an Australian swimming champion.

Andrew 'Boy' Charlton won an Olympic Gold Medal for the 1500 m freestyle in 1924.

The first Australian Olympic swimmer was Freddy Lane in Paris, 1900.

The 2000 Olympic Games were held in Sydney.

Ian Thorpe is one of Australia's all time greatest swimmers.

3 Underline the **verb group** in each sentence.

The first modern Olympics was held in Athens in 1896.

Australia has been competing in Olympic swimming since 1900.

Murray Rose is recognised as one of Australia's finest swimmers.

Olympic champion Dawn Fraser was born in 1937.

Australian swimmers have proven their ability in international competition.

4 Change each **verb form** to show that the action happened in the past.

We (run) ________________ to catch the bus.

I (hop) ________________ over the fence.

Minnie (says) ________________ to hurry up.

Johnny (reads) ________________ at bed time.

Trai (chops) ________________ the carrots.

5 Write **past**, **present** or **future** after each sentence to show when the event will, or did, take place.

We caught the ferry. ______________

I will catch the ferry. ______________

I am catching the ferry. ______________

I am on the telephone. ______________

I was on the telephone. ______________

I will phone her tomorrow. ______________

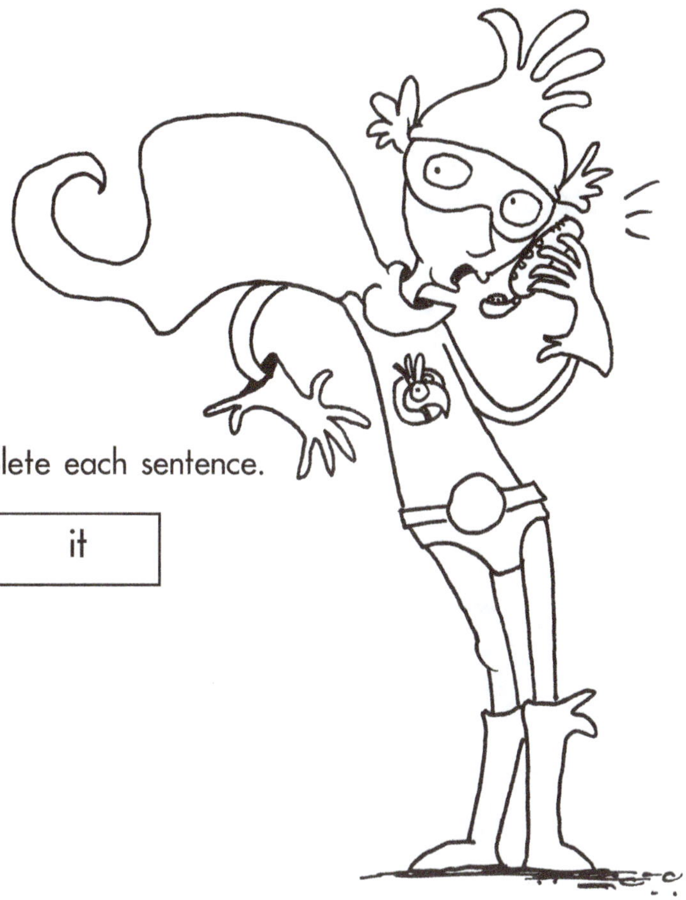

6 Choose a **personal pronoun** from the box to complete each sentence.

us	I	you	it

________ like to watch the Olympics.

Mum gives ________ pocket money for jobs.

Put ________ in the cupboard.

Will ________ return the book to the library?

7 Choose the correct **comparative** and **superlative adjectives** from the box to complete each sentence.

bigger	biggest	slower	slowest	funnier	funniest

The tortoise is ______________ than the hare.

I read the ______________ book.

This book is ______________ than the other one.

The tortoise is the ______________ runner in the zoo.

My feet are ______________ than yours.

His teeth are the ______________.

8 Write *more* or *most* on the lines.

One fish was ______________ colourful than the other.

This is the ______________ colourful fish.

The Kimberley is one of the ______________ remote regions of Australia.

Antarctica is ______________ remote than the Kimberley.

This informative text is an **information report**. The **noun groups** form word chains called **lexical chains**.

Sewage

If you live in a city or town, your home is probably connected to the sewerage system. Sewage is the name for all the used water and waste that goes down the plugholes in your home. These plugholes include your toilet, kitchen sink, washing machine, dishwasher, bathroom sinks, showers and bathtubs. Sewage leaves your home and is collected in the sewerage system. It is then transferred to a treatment plant. After treatment, sewage can be reused.

In places where there is no sewerage system, the waste can be collected in septic tanks.

Rule! **Lexical chains** are made up of words that link a particular content strand in a text. A lexical chain about dogs could be:
kinds of dogs *spotty Dalmatians* *tired old daschunds* *energetic beagles*

1 Read *Sewage*. Circle and link the words that make a **lexical chain** related to sewage and the sewerage system.

2 Now list the words that make a **lexical chain** for things in the home.

____

____

3 Write a lexical chain of **noun groups** for things that use or contain water in your home.

____

____

4 Write a lexical chain of at least five **doing verbs** for things that you can do with water.

____

____

5 Use a dictionary to find definitions for the **technical terms** used in *Sewage*.

sewage: ____

sewerage: ____

Rule! **Commas** are used to separate items in a list of nouns. The word *and* is usually used instead of a comma between the last two items.

6 Complete these lists of items. Use **commas** between each item and the word *and* between the last two items.

Four types of fruit are oranges, ________________, ________________ and ________________.

Four marine animals are ____

Three toys to use in the water are ____

____

7 Write a sentence that contains a list of **nouns** for five water sports. Remember to use **commas**.

____

____

____

8 Underline the **theme** in each sentence.

Wash your hands after using the toilet.

Thoroughly wash your hands before eating.

Germs can make you sick.

Flush the toilet after use.

Try it yourself!

Design a poster for display in the school toilet block. Include a set of instructions to remind students to flush after use and wash their hands with soap. Use a different colour for the **lexical chain** of nouns.

Reflection

- I can do this.
- I am not sure.
- I need help.

Unit **26** Verb groups, conjunctions

How a Pearl is Made

Pearls are made by pearl oysters.

It all begins when the ocean currents wash a tiny grain of sand or grit inside the oyster's shell. This small piece of foreign material then irritates the oyster, so the oyster begins to coat it with mucus called nacre.

The oyster keeps adding layers of nacre around the sharp grit until it becomes smooth. This is the pearl. But still it irritates the oyster. Therefore the oyster keeps adding more and more layers, making the pearl bigger and bigger.

This informative text is an **explanation**. It uses **conjunctions** to link parts of the text in a time sequence and to show cause and effect.

1 Read *How a Pearl is Made*. Underline the **verb groups**.

2 Tick a box to show when the action happened.

	Past	Present	Future
The oyster made a pearl.	☐	☐	☐
Oysters make pearls.	☐	☐	☐
The oysters will make pearls.	☐	☐	☐
My pearl was made by an oyster.	☐	☐	☐
Otters eat oysters.	☐	☐	☐
I hope the otter doesn't swallow the pearl.	☐	☐	☐
The oyster is stuck to the rock.	☐	☐	☐

3 In *How a Pearl is Made* find three **conjunctions** that link events in a time sequence.

________________ ________________ ________________

Tip! Remember the rule on page 50.

Now find two **conjunctions** that link events through cause and effect.

________________________ ________________________

Finally, find a **conjunction** that links ideas by adding them.

____

4 Choose a **conjunction** from the box to finish each sentence.

when	after	because	however

Pearls are very valuable ________________ they grow so slowly.

Pearls can be found in nature; ________________, they are very rare.

Cultured pearls are made ________________ a person places a piece of shell into an oyster.

________________ two years a pearl can measure 8 mm.

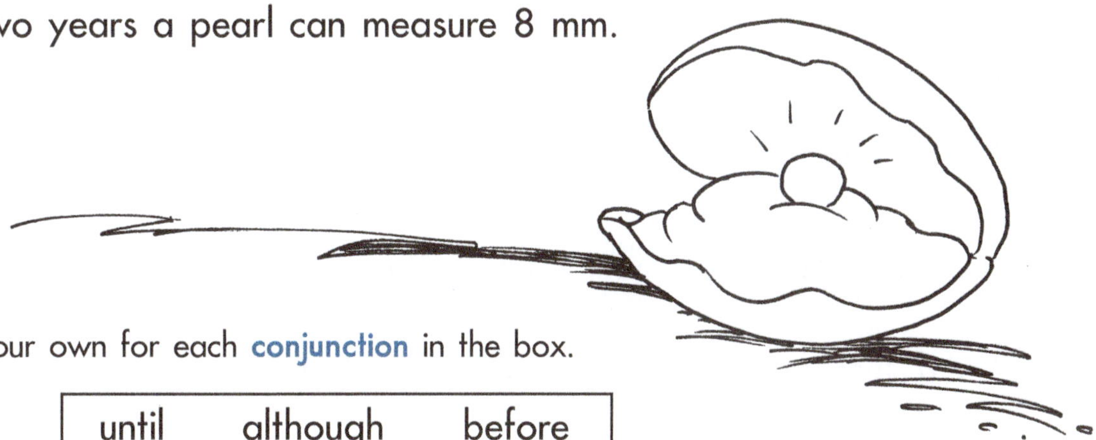

5 Write a sentence of your own for each **conjunction** in the box.

until	although	before

____

____

____

Try it yourself!

Write an **explanation** about something that interests you. Write in present tense. Ask a peer to help edit your work.

Reflection

- I can do this.
- I am not sure.
- I need help.

Unit 27

Reference chains, classifying adjectives

This informative text is an **information report**. It connects information across the text with the noun-pronoun **reference chain** for cane toads.

Cane Toads

Cane toads were imported to Australia from Hawaii in 1935. They were introduced to Queensland sugar cane farms to eat the cane beetles that were destroying sugar cane crops. Cane toads have now successfully spread across the top of Australia, covering an area of more than one million square kilometres.

Cane toads eat anything they can swallow. Australian indigenous animals, such as snakes, lizards and water birds, are poisoned and killed when they attempt to eat the cane toad. Cane toads have no predators in nature.

Rule! **Reference chains** are made up of words used throughout a text that refer to the same person, place, animal or thing.

1 Read *Cane Toads*. Circle the words that are part of the **reference chain** referring to the cane toads.

2 Words that are part of the cane toad **reference chain** are in **theme** position in every sentence except one. Write the sentence that has a different **theme**. Circle the **theme**.

____

____

3 Why do you think the author gave this sentence a different theme?

____

____

4 Underline the **proper nouns** in *Cane Toads*.

Rule!

Classifying adjectives classify, or tell the group that a **noun** or **pronoun** belongs to.

cane toad

To test if an adjective is a **classifying adjective**, try to add the word *very* in front of it. It won't make sense.

a very hammerhead shark

5 Find three **noun groups** in *Cane Toads* that contain **classifying adjectives**.

____

____

6 Underline the **adjectives** in the **noun groups** below. Then circle the **classifying adjectives**.

a long tennis match

a big humpback whale

webbed hind feet

Australian marsupials

South Pacific Islands

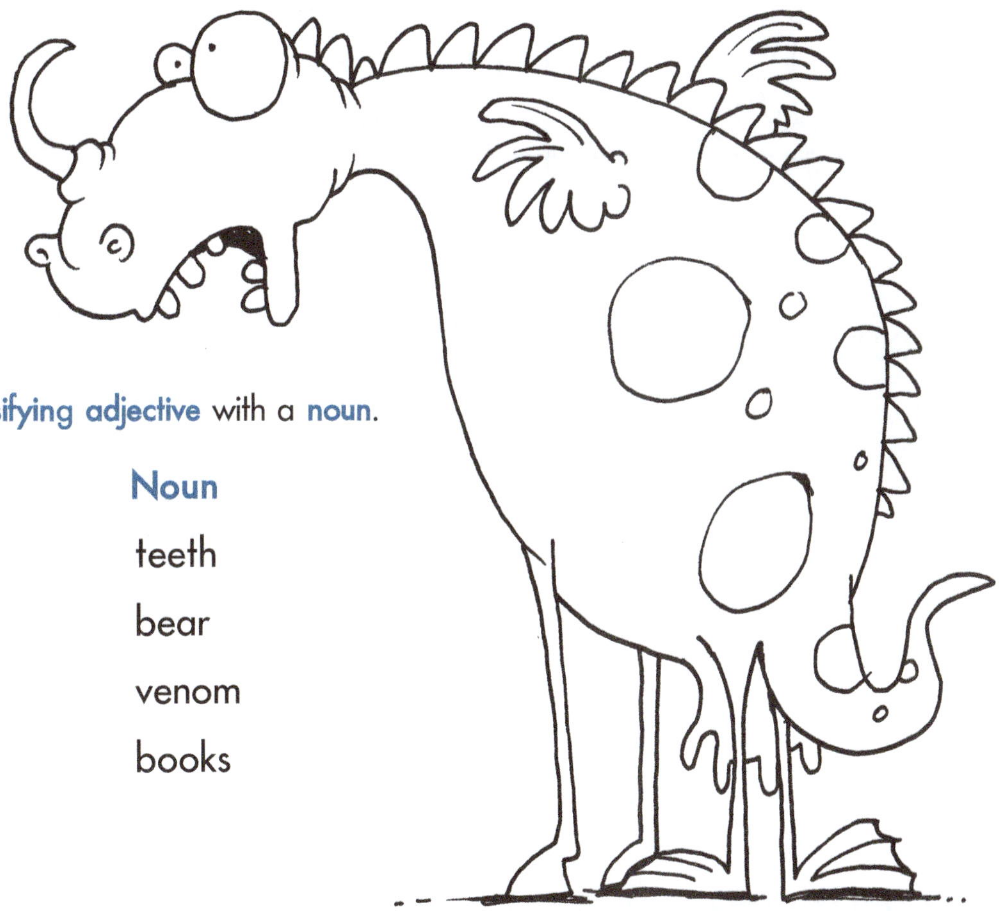

7 Draw a line to match each **classifying adjective** with a **noun**.

Classifying adjective	Noun
library	teeth
polar	bear
snake	venom
shark	books

Try it yourself!

Do some research about another feral animal. Write an **information report** to share with your class. Use a **reference chain** to link information through the text. Add internet images and create a short slide show to present the information to the class.

Reflection

- I can do this.
- I am not sure.
- I need help.

Unit 28

Question tags, verbs, conjunctions

This **discussion** includes persuasive **statements** that present different points of view.

WHAT'S YOUR FAVOURITE SEA ANIMAL?

Chairperson: Today, we are discussing sea animals.

Ali: My favourite sea animal is the humpback whale. I love the way they look after their babies and they are so playful and inquisitive. You love them too, don't you, Ben?

Ben: Yes. I like humpbacks, but my favourite sea animal is the white pointer shark because it is the boss of the ocean. It's fierce, intelligent and an incredible predator, don't you think?

Ali: Yes, I agree with you that white pointers are amazing; however, my favourite is still the humpback whale. I'm sure they are more intelligent than sharks so we should do everything we can to protect them from whaling.

Chairperson: Well, it sounds like humpback whales and white pointer sharks are very different creatures. There are admirable things about both species.

Tip! **Questions** are sometimes formed by adding a **question tag** to the end of a **statement** or **command**.
You love them too, don't you?

1 Read *What's Your Favourite Sea Animal?* What **question** does Ben ask that has a **question tag**?

____

Why does Ben use this form of questioning?

____

2 Add a **question tag** to each **statement** or **command** to turn it into a **question**.

I'm allowed to go. I'm allowed to go, aren't I?

You're coming. ______________________________

I can have it. ______________________________

You will give me one. ______________________________

3 Circle the thinking and feeling verbs in *What's Your Favourite Sea Animal?*

4 Write a sentence to tell how you think or feel about whales or sharks. Use a different thinking and feeling verb to the ones you circled in question 3.

____

____

5 Use a conjunction from the box to join each pair of sentences. Tick the column to show the function of the conjunction in each sentence.

Tip! Remember the rule on page 50.

so	because	however	but

	Function	
	to compare	to show one thing causes another
I love whales. I don't like eels. ________________		
Whales breed in warmer water. Whales migrate from Antarctica up the coast of Australia. ________________ ________________		
I like sharks. I prefer whales. ________________		
I love whales. They are gentle giants. ________________		

6 In *What's Your Favourite Sea Animal?*, Ben and Ali each use two conjunctions to show connections in their arguments. Write them on the lines.

Ben ________________ ________________

Ali ________________ ________________

Try it yourself!

Have a discussion with a partner about your favourite animals. Each of you needs to offer two reasons for the animal being your favourite. Use conjunctions to show connections in your reasons. Use thinking and feeling verbs. Write a transcript of the discussion.

Reflection

- I can do this.
- I am not sure.
- I need help.

Unit 29

Noun groups, adjectives, subject-verb agreement

This persuasive text is a **response**. It uses **thinking and feeling verbs** and **adjectives**.

Daintree

The Daintree area in North Queensland is a great travel destination. The Daintree Rainforest meets the ocean at the Great Barrier Reef. Half-day and whole-day guided walks in the 135-million-year-old rainforest are available. The number of plant, tree and bird species will amaze you. You might be really lucky and see a cassowary. Cassowaries are flightless birds that live in the Daintree but they are endangered so they are pretty rare. I love the Daintree Rainforest and I am sure you will love it too. I give it four stars as a school holiday destination for families.

Tip! Remember the rule on page 12.

1 Read *Daintree*. Write the **noun groups** that refer to places, animals and things.

Places	Animals	Things

2 Write the **adjectives** used in *Daintree*.

3 Write **adjectives** of your own to describe a great holiday that you have had or would like to have.

Rule!

The subject of a **clause** and the **verb** need to agree in number.
Plural number: *The sharks live. They live.*
Singular number: *It lives. The shark lives.*

4 Rewrite each sentence. Change the underlined **noun** to **singular**. Remember to also change the **verb** to match. Say the new sentences out loud to make sure the words sound right.

The <u>children</u> run past the teachers. → The child runs past the teachers.

The <u>dogs</u> eat sausages. ____________________

The <u>babies</u> cry for hours. ____________________

The <u>authors</u> visit all schools in the district. ____________________

5 Underline the four **thinking and feeling verb groups** used in *Daintree*.

6 After reading *Daintree* would you like to visit there? Give a reason for your opinion. Use a **thinking and feeling verb**.

Try it yourself!

Write a **response** to a place you have visited, like a friend's home, a park, the beach or anywhere else. Use **verbs** that tell how you think and feel about the place. Include **noun groups** with **adjectives**.

Reflection

- I can do this.
- I am not sure.
- I need help.

Unit 30 Revision

1 Circle the words in this passage that form a **lexical chain** about the topic of clothes.

Yesterday, Harry and I got our new soccer uniforms. Our boots and shorts got muddy during the match, so we had to change into clean jeans and shoes afterwards. We kept our jerseys on all day.

2 Circle all the words in this sentence that form a **reference chain** referring to the cat.

The cat lived a double life. It curled up on the sofa every afternoon, purring sweetly. At night, it prowled the alleys, looking for a fight.

3 Underline the **theme** in each sentence.

After a long time we came to a lake.

The blue whale is the largest whale.

The largest whale is the blue whale.

The lake came into view after a long walk.

4 Write lists with **commas** and the word *and.*

Four vegetables: ______________________________

Three teachers: ______________________________

Five colours: ______________________________

5 Underline the **classifying adjective** in each **noun group**.

an exciting boat ride

a small baby octopus

big hind legs

difficult computer game

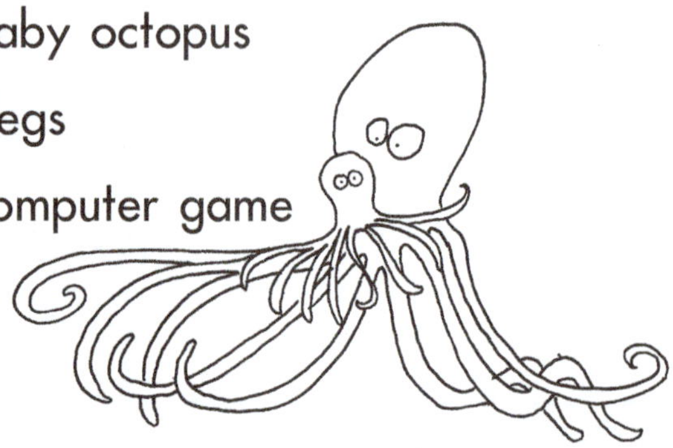

6 Write *question, statement* or *command* after each sentence and use the correct punctuation marks.

You'll be late ______________________

You'll be late, won't you ______________________

Don't be late ______________________

Will you be late ______________________

I hope you're not late ______________________

7 Use a **conjunction** from the box to complete each sentence.

but	until	and	so	because

Uncle Hal can't eat sugar ________________ we bought him artificial sweetener.

Meg will wait ________________ Pia has finished dinner.

Leila ________________ Eric are coming to dinner.

Hugo likes broccoli ________________ Ireni doesn't.

I'll stay inside ________________ it's raining.

8 Write **adverbs** that tell how.

Please walk ________________ on the slippery floor.

Run ________________ to the finish line.

Walk ________________ to balance the egg on the spoon.

Work ________________ during the test.

Sit ________________ during the assembly.

9 Rewrite each sentence using a **plural noun**. Remember to use the matching **verbs**.

The child runs past the teacher.

____

The baby cries for an hour.

____

The dog eats a bone.

____

The author visits the school.

____

10 Rewrite each sentence with correct punctuation. Don't forget to begin **proper nouns** with a capital letter.

my friend gemma is travelling to north queensland for the school holidays in december

____

____

the great barrier reef marine park is beautiful

____

cassowaries live at cape tribulation

____

Unit 31

Verb groups, verb forms

This informative text is an information report. It uses verb groups to show actions and relationships.

Tsunami

A tsunami is a big wave. Tsunamis are mainly caused by earthquakes in the sea floor. They can also occur when a volcano erupts. When Mount Krakatoa erupted in Indonesia in 1883, it caused a tsunami that grew to 40 metres high on the coast of Indonesia. When that tsunami reached the north-west coast of Australia it was still six metres high.

Tsunami waves quickly move out and away from where the earthquake or volcano occurred. Sometimes there's only one tsunami. Sometimes there's a series of tsunamis. The north-west coast of Australia is the most likely place on Australia's coast to be hit by a tsunami.

1 Read *Tsunami*. It contains these verb groups.

is are mainly caused erupted caused can also occur
reached was move to be hit erupts

Tip! Remember the rule on page 24.

Write each verb group in the correct column.

Relating verb groups	Doing verb groups

2 Circle two **adverbs** in *Tsunami*. Use each of them in a sentence of your own.

____

____

Rule!

All **verbs** have a **base form**. *erupt*
The suffix *–ing* can turn verbs into **present tense**. *erupting*
The suffix *–ed* or *–d* can turn some verbs into **past tense**. *erupted*
These are **regular verbs**.

3 Add **suffixes** to write the different forms of these **regular verbs**.

Base form	Present tense	Past tense
play	I am ________	I ________
walk	I am ________	I ________
receive	I am ________	I ________
laugh	I am ________	I ________

Rule!

Some verbs form the past tense in different ways than adding *–ed*. These are called **irregular verbs** because they do not follow a regular pattern.
grow *grew*

4 Write the different forms of these **irregular verbs**.

Base form	Present tense	Past tense
fly	I am ________	I ________
take	I am ________	I ________
fight	I am ________	I ________
drink	I am ________	I ________
teach	I am ________	I ________

Try it yourself!

A tsunami is different from a tidal wave. Research tidal waves and write an **information report**. Create a poster to present the information to the class.

Reflection

- I can do this.
- I am not sure.
- I need help.

Unit 32

Speech, modality, emotive words

This informative text is a newspaper article. It uses **quoted** (direct) and **reported** (indirect) **speech** to show what was said.

High Tide Sends Residents to the Roof

Residents of Bilkington were forced to abandon their homes and head for their roofs yesterday as a combination of high tide, heavy rains and a storm surge meant many of their homes went underwater. Local resident, Ted Egan, said he had advised Wickham Council last year that the council's drainage system would not cope with the amount of run-off that would result from a tropical cyclone combining with a high tide. His daughter, Terri, sat on their roof yesterday and shouted, "No school today!"

Tip! **Emotive** words are emotional. A writer may use them to make the reader feel a certain way.

1 Read *High Tide Sends Residents to the Roof*. What **emotive** words are used in the first sentence?

____

2 Replace the underlined words with more **emotive** words.

The red team was <u>beaten</u>. ______________________

The people <u>had</u> to walk a long way. ______________________

The shopkeeper <u>overcharged</u> the customer. ______________________

3 Re-read *High Tide Sends Residents to the Roof*. Underline the **reported speech**. Circle the **quoted speech**.

4 Change the **quoted speech** to **reported speech**.

Terri said, "My teacher will miss me."

____

Tip! Remember the rules on pages 42 and 43.

Mary Egan said, "Ted warned the council to look out for the next cyclone season."

____

5 Rewrite these sentences with correct punctuation.

wickham council member deanne cole said we will investigate the matter further

____

gee I wish I could go to school terri egan complained

____

terris brother told me he thought the flood was good fun

____

mary egan said I managed to rescue my cat budgie photo albums and handbag before climbing up to the roof

____

____

> **Tip!**
>
> **Modal verbs** can tell you the degree of certainty the speaker or writer has about something. This is called **modality**.
>
> **High modality** means certain. *will* *will not*
>
> **Low modality** means uncertain. *might* *might not*

6 Rewrite each sentence with **lower modality** to express less certainty.

The drains will not cope with the run-off. ______________________

The council should do something. ______________________

Homes will be ruined. ______________________

People will be angry. ______________________

People should not give up hope. ______________________

Try it yourself!

Write an information report in the form of a **newspaper article** about an incident that could occur in your local area. Use **quoted** and **reported speech**. Use **emotive language**. Use **modal verbs** to express **modality**.

Reflection

- I can do this.
- I am not sure.
- I need help.

Quoted (direct) and reported (indirect) speech; modality; modal verbs: *will, will not, might, might not, should, should not*; emotive language

Unit **33** Connecting arguments, modality

This persuasive text is an **exposition**. It presents one point of view. It uses **connectives** to link ideas. It uses **high modality**.

Vote Against School Swimming

I do not think that swimming should be a compulsory school sport. Firstly, I believe that anyone in Australia who wants to swim or who likes swimming will swim outside of school anyway, so why waste school time doing things that everyone can already do? A second reason for voting against compulsory swimming in schools is the risk of skin cancer in Australia. We should not be expecting school children to spend any time in the sun at swimming pools. In addition, I feel that the time spent at swimming would be better spent doing other more important indoor activities like spelling and grammar.

1 Read *Vote Against School Swimming*. Summarise the three reasons the writer expresses for not swimming at school.

____

____

____

____

____

Rule!

Connectives link ideas through a text.
Connectives can be **conjunctions**.
and *or* *so*
Connectives can also be words that link or **sequence** arguments.
firstly *secondly* *in addition*

2 In *Vote Against School Swimming* underline the words that help to **sequence** the arguments.

Tip! Remember the rule on page 10.

3 Write the **thinking and feeling verbs** used in *Vote Against School Swimming*.

____

4 Place a tick in the column for **high** or **low modality** for each sentence.

	High modality	Low modality
We must hurry.		
We might be late.		
We should walk faster.		
You are not allowed in.		

Tip! Remember the rule on page 69.

5 In *Vote Against School Swimming* circle the **modal verbs** that show **modality**. Remember these are words that express how certain the writer is of something.

6 Write an **exposition** in favour of compulsory school swimming. Use **connectives** to link your arguments. Use **thinking and feeling verbs**, and **high modality**.

Try it yourself!

Write an **exposition** for or against something you feel strongly about. Use **connectives** like *firstly* and *secondly* to structure your argument. Use **high modality** words like *must* and *should* to show you are certain of your opinions. Use **thinking and feeling verbs** to express your opinions.

Reflection

- I can do this.
- I am not sure.
- I need help.

Connectives: *firstly, secondly, in addition*; modality; modal verbs: *might, should, could, must*; thinking and feeling verbs

Unit 34 Prepositional phrases, adverbs

This imaginative text is the orientation of a **narrative**. It uses **prepositional phrases** and **adverbs** to set the scene.

Bobby and the Quest for the Hidden Treasure

Once upon a time there lived a frog called Bobby, who lived at the bottom of the swamp. One day, Bobby and his friends decided to go on a quest. Bobby remembered hearing his family talk about a treasure that was supposedly under a huge willow tree, inside a waterfall, so they set off to find it. After travelling for a while, they heard the roaring sound of water and hopped towards it. They looked up and saw a huge waterfall. The frogs hopped through the cascading water into a cave on the other side, and found an enormous willow tree. Hurriedly, they began to dig under it.

1 Read *Bobby and the Quest for the Hidden Treasure.* Find the **prepositional phrases** that tell where.

Tip! Remember the rule on page 31.

____

____

____

____

2 Complete each sentence with a **prepositional phrase** to tell where.

I sat ____.

I found it ____.

He lived ____.

We ran ____.

It rolled ____.

3 Complete each sentence with a **prepositional phrase** that tells when.

Captain Swashbuckle had a nap ______________________________.

We'll go ______________________________.

______________________________ I went surfing.

______________________________ we'll see the lighthouse.

The museum is open ______________________________.

> **Tip!** Using different word groups in **theme** position can surprise a reader and keep the story interesting.

4 Write **prepositional phrases** that tell when or where for the beginning of each sentence.

______________________________ they heard the roaring sound of water.

______________________________ they heard the roaring sound of water.

______________________________ they heard the roaring sound of water.

______________________________ they heard the roaring sound of water.

______________________________ they heard the roaring sound of water.

5 Write an **adverb** that tells how in **theme** position in each sentence.
Hint! Adverbs often end in *–ly*.

______________________, he sat down on the mountain peak.

______________________, she crossed through the room.

______________________, they trudged for hours through the dunes.

______________________, they photographed the bilby before it hopped away.

______________________, the humpback cavorted in the ocean depths.

Try it yourself!

Write an ending for *Bobby and the Quest for the Hidden Treasure*. What treasure did the frogs discover and how did they get it home? Include **prepositional phrases** that tell where and when and **adverbs** that tell how.

Reflection

- I can do this.
- I am not sure.
- I need help.

Unit

35 Revision

1 Complete the chart.

Base form	Past tense	Regular/irregular
see	I ______________	______________
buy	I ______________	______________
jump	I ______________	______________
tickle	I ______________	______________
think	I ______________	______________

2 Rewrite each sentence with correct punctuation and capital letters.

I love swimming at school exclaimed david

____

why can't we swim every day asked poppy

____

it wastes too much time replied tom

____

that's the whole idea said rachael

____

3 Replace the underlined words with **higher modality** words.

The drains might not cope with the run-off.

____

The council might be able to do something.

____

Homes could be ruined. ______________________

People may be upset. ______________________

4 Underline the **connectives**.

I don't like television. First of all, I get bored just sitting on the couch. Secondly, the ads are really annoying. Finally, there's never any good shows on!

5 Complete each sentence with a **verb** or **verb group**.

We ________________________ because it's nearly Christmas!

The tugboat ________________________ triumphantly over the waves.

She ________________________ a real chatterbox.

I strapped on my waterskis and ________________________ along the river.

I ________________________ it's too chilly to go for a swim.

You ________________________ my best friend.

6 Write a **prepositional phrase** to tell where.

They crossed ____.

I looked ____.

Ned found a sea star ____.

She threw it ____.

We swam ____.

7 Write a **prepositional phrase** to tell when.

____ we played at the rockpool.

Johan likes a cup of tea ____.

We watch the football ____.

The dentist will see you ____.

____ I completed my quest.

8 Write an **adverb** in **theme** position.

____________________, the lorikeets squabbled over food.

____________________ remove the dish from the oven.

____________________ pull out the thorn.

____________________ finish this book!

Grammar Rules

Look at the page number in the star to find more information about the rule.

adjective .... a word that tells you more about a **noun**

classifying adjective 59

comparative and superlative adjective 51

descriptive adjective 18

number adjective 20

possessive adjective (a word that shows ownership) 23

adverb .... a word that adds meaning to a **verb**, **adjective** or another **adverb**. Adverbs can tell how, when or where.

*adding meaning to **verbs** by telling how* 34

clause .... a group of words that expresses an idea and contains a **verb** 27

command .... a sentence that tells someone to do something 33

conjunction .... a joining word that links ideas in a **sentence**.

Conjunctions are **connectives**. 11 27

adding information 50

comparing things 50

showing one thing causes another 50

showing a time sequence 50

connective .... a word or words that link ideas through a text 70

lexical chain .... a chain of words that link a particular content strand in a text 54

modality .... the degree of certainty the speaker or writer has about something. **High modality** is certain, **low modality** is uncertain. 69

noun .... a word for a person, place or thing 6

collective noun 21

common noun 8

noun group 12 23 36

proper noun 8

singular and plural 21 63